LONDON 1967

A Photo Essay

Copyright: © 2015 Bob Bovin, Ninni Bovin
Bovin Design Hb, Lilla Nygatan 15, Stockholm
Homepage: www.bovin.nu/bob
E-mail: bob@bovin.nu

Print and distribution: createspace, an Amazon company.

ISBN 978-91978005-9-4

LONDON 1967

A Photo Essay

by
Bob and Ninni Bovin

The summer of London 1967

Events

The United Kingdom and Ireland officially applied for European Economic Community membership.

The first automatic cash machine (voucher-based) was installed in the office of Barclays Bank in Enfield.

The first scheduled colour television broadcasts from six transmitters covering the main population centers in England began.

Parliament decriminalized male homosexuality in England and Wales with the Sexual Offences Act.

The British steel industry was nationalized.

Pink Floyd released their debut album The Piper at the Gates of Dawn.

Dunlop Valley entered the UK Weather Records with the highest 90-min total rainfall at 117 mm.

The UK Marine Broadcasting Offences Act declared participation in offshore pirate radio illegal.

BBC Radio 1 was launched.

Pink Floyd staged the first ever rock concert with quadraphonic sound at Queen Elizabeth Hall, London

Paul McCartney met the American photographer Linda Eastman at a club called "Bag O' Nails".

Sgt. Pepper's Lonely Hearts Club Band by The Beatles was released in mono and stereo versions.

At the start of the 20th Aldeburgh Festival, Queen Elizabeth II of the United Kingdom opened the new Snape Maltings concert hall.

The Beatles performed "All You Need Is Love" for the Our World television special, the first worldwide television broadcast.

The Monkees flow into London at the start of their concerts at the Empire Pool, Wembley.

Mick Jagger and Keith Richards were sentenced to jail for drug possession. They later appealed successfully against the sentences.

Our London in 1967

It is easy to romanticize the good old days, with new music in the streets and the new fashion seen in Carnaby Street. That summer Ninni and I came to London. The mind was bright and confidence was there. This was not only a time of hustle and bustle. It was also a time of strong tensions between the countries of the world. England had not fully recovered after World War II. Europe had rose from the ashes. The music was playfully happy. The fashionable pastel colored skirts were over the knee short. On the streets there were musicians.

That was before the vegetable market, Covent Garden became a tourist trap. There were still hard work of transshipment and transportation, and wholesale trade. Among all men, women were rarely seen here, there were even children who drove carts. We took the subway to Covent Garden several days and we thought it was fun to see the process of loading and unloading of horticultural products and flowers.

It was toast and bacon for breakfast with fried sausages and eggs. Everything was served by tuxedo dressed men. The hotel was not a luxury one, but a pretty little house sandwiched among three-story houses. I had to change the shirt every day because the collar was black by smoke in the air.

Our strolling around in this city for many weeks, with our cameras, Minolta SR7 and Leica M2, led to quite a number of interesting photographs in black and white or color. We have selected out some photos from this London, and it's not the shiny glossy bank palaces we see today.

Bob and Ninni

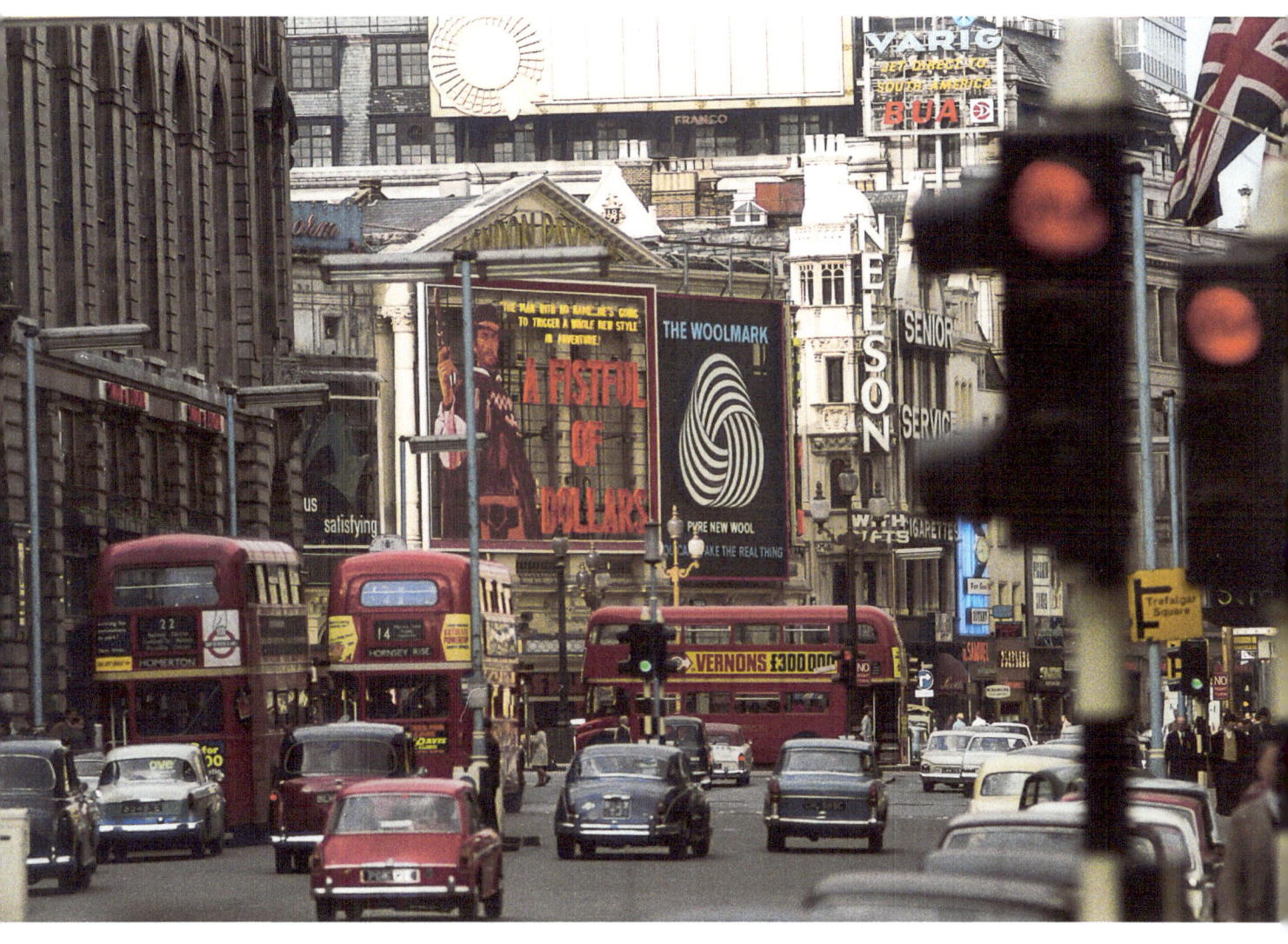

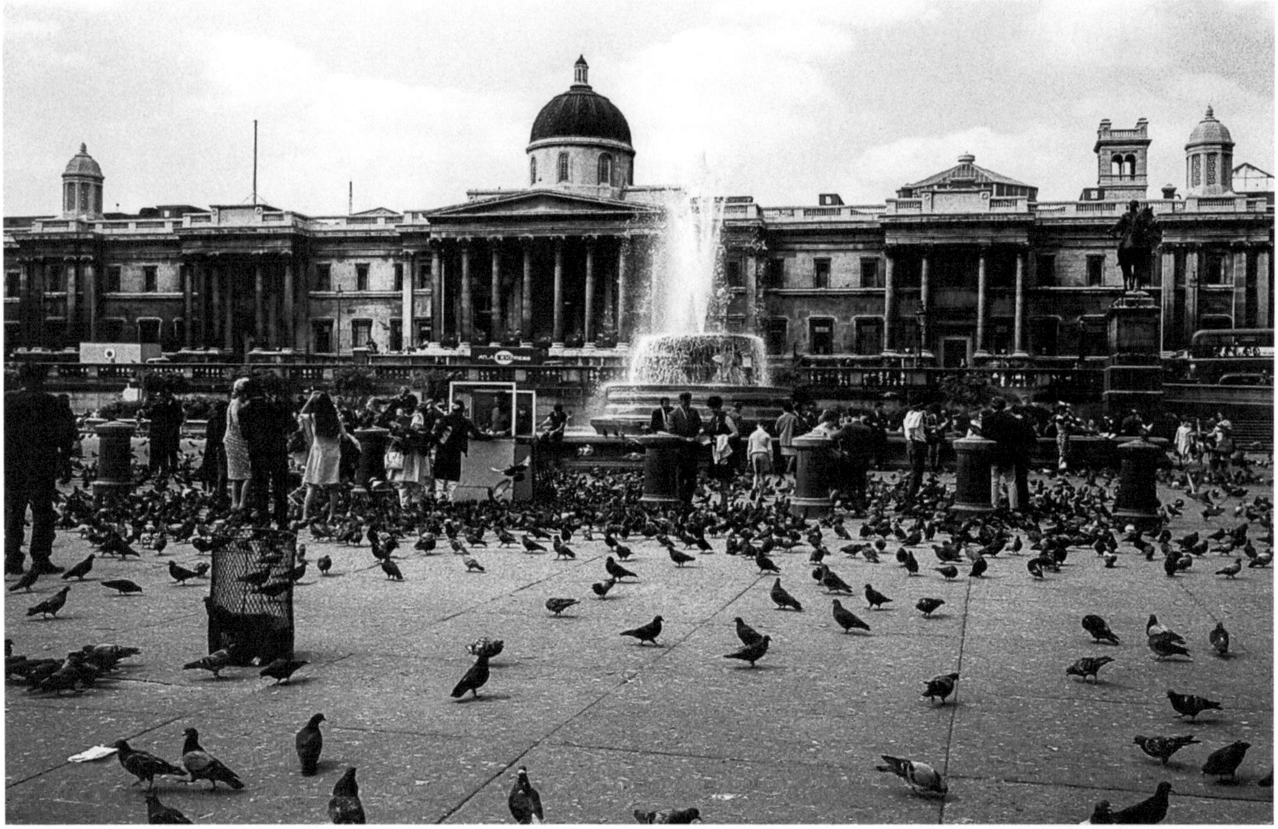

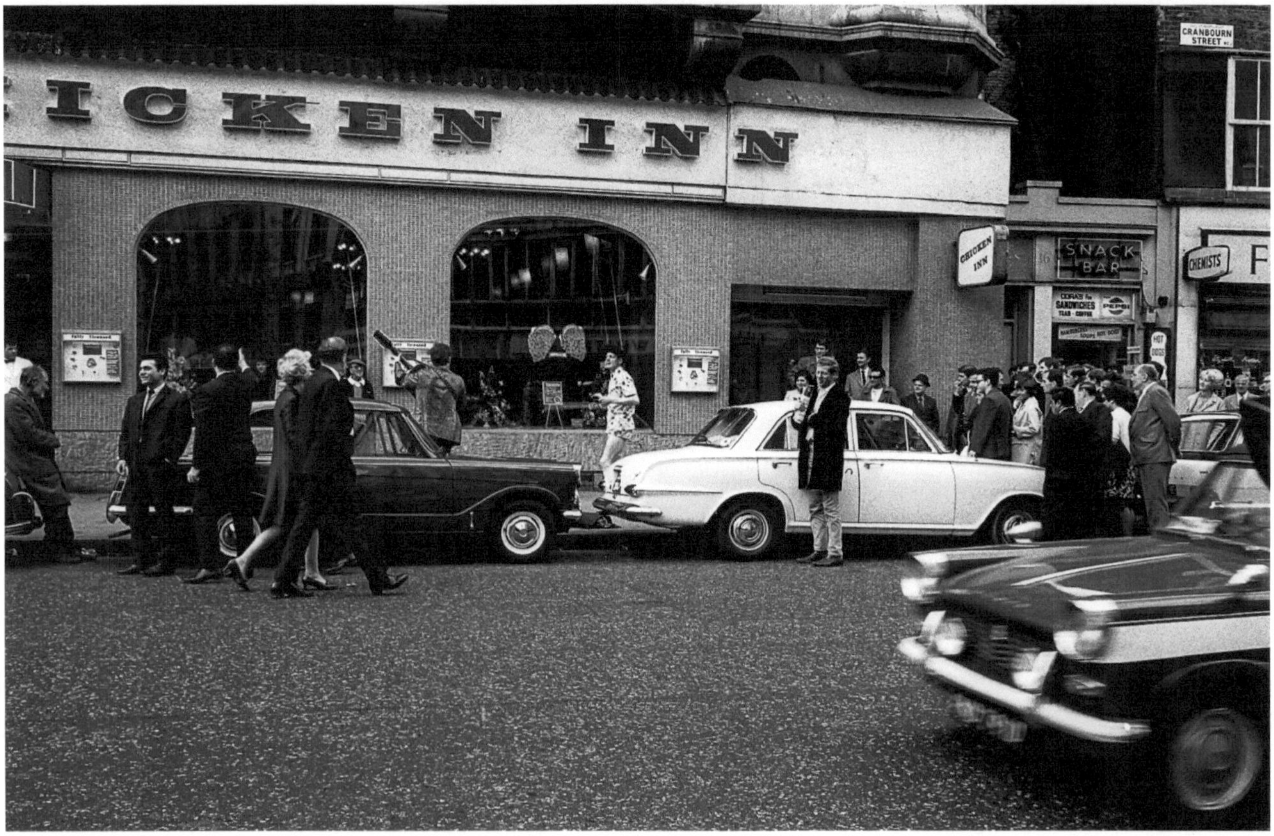

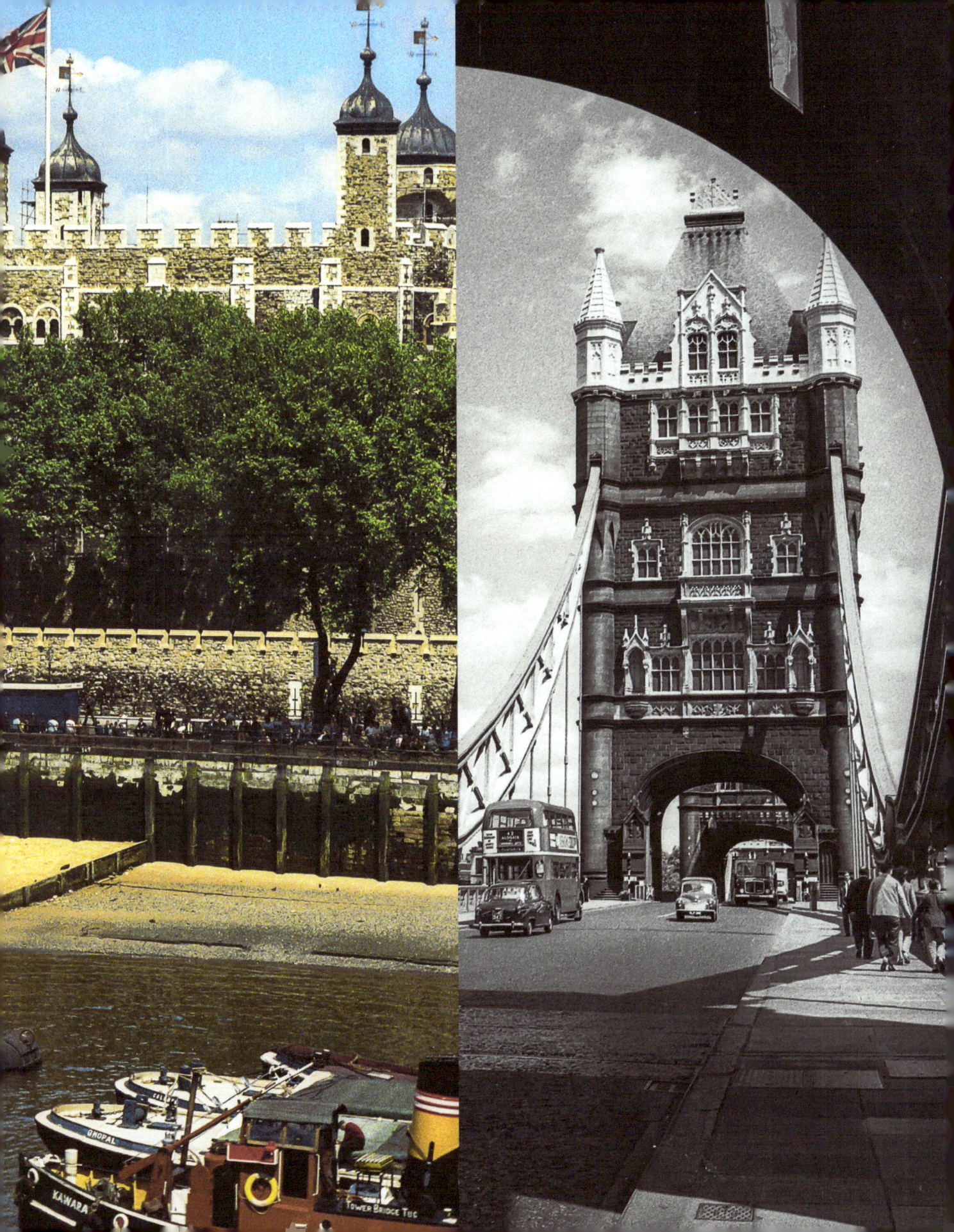

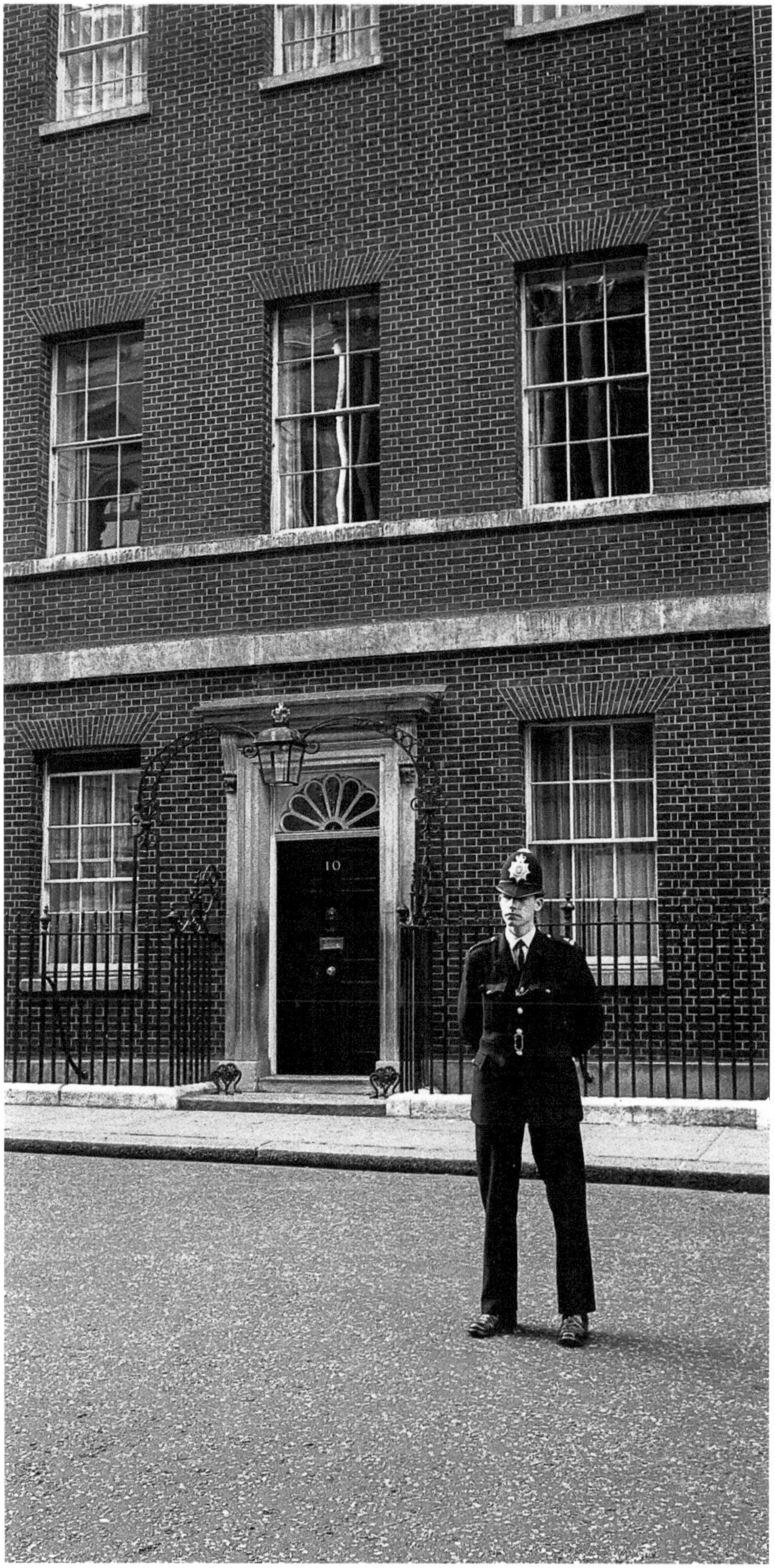

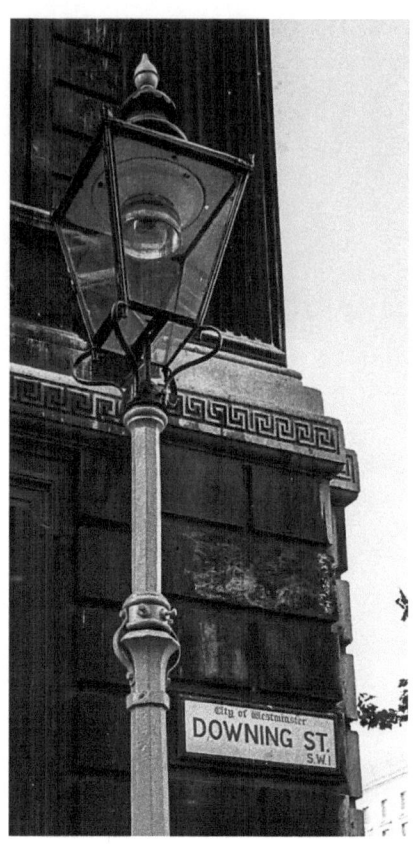

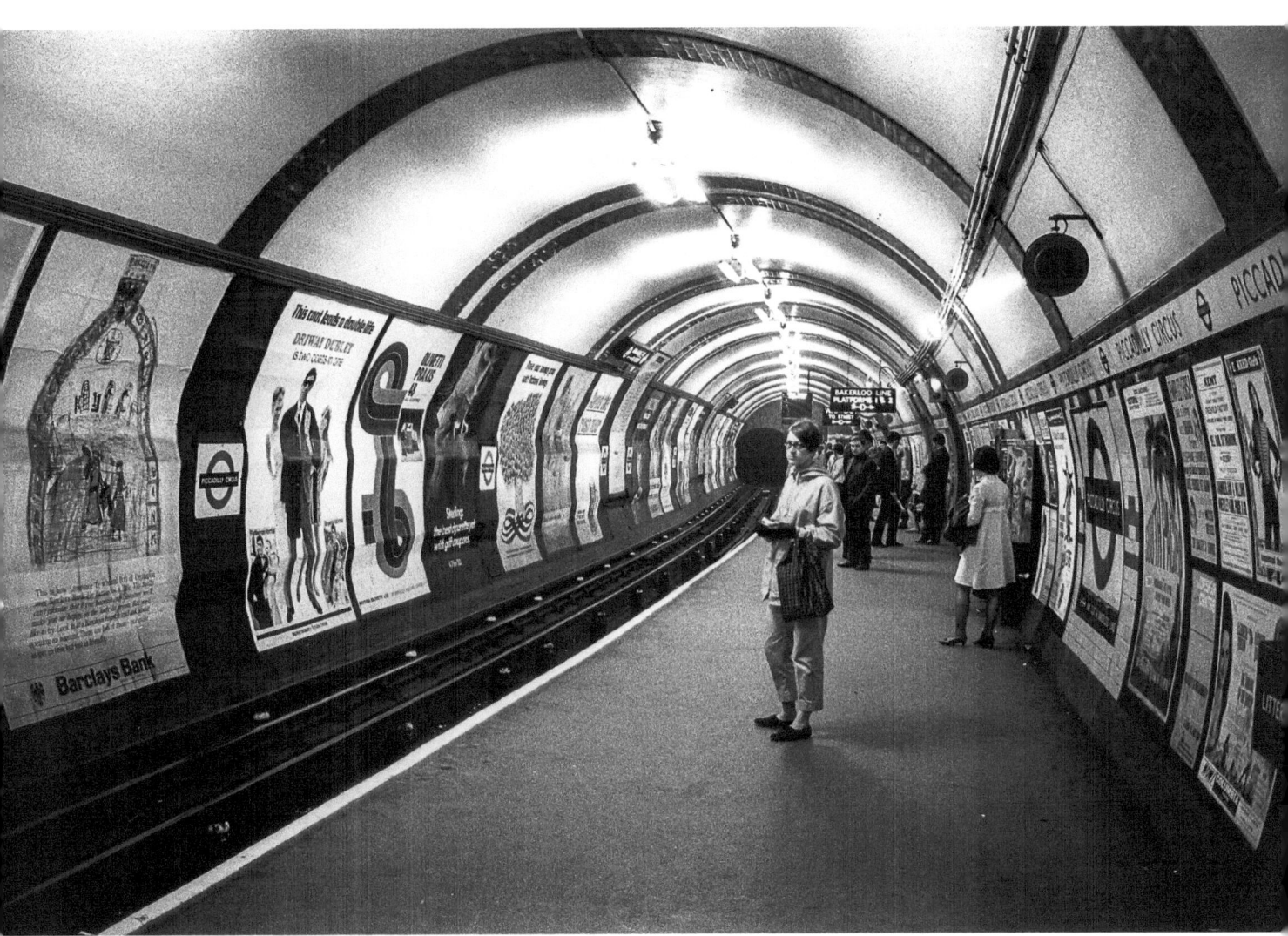

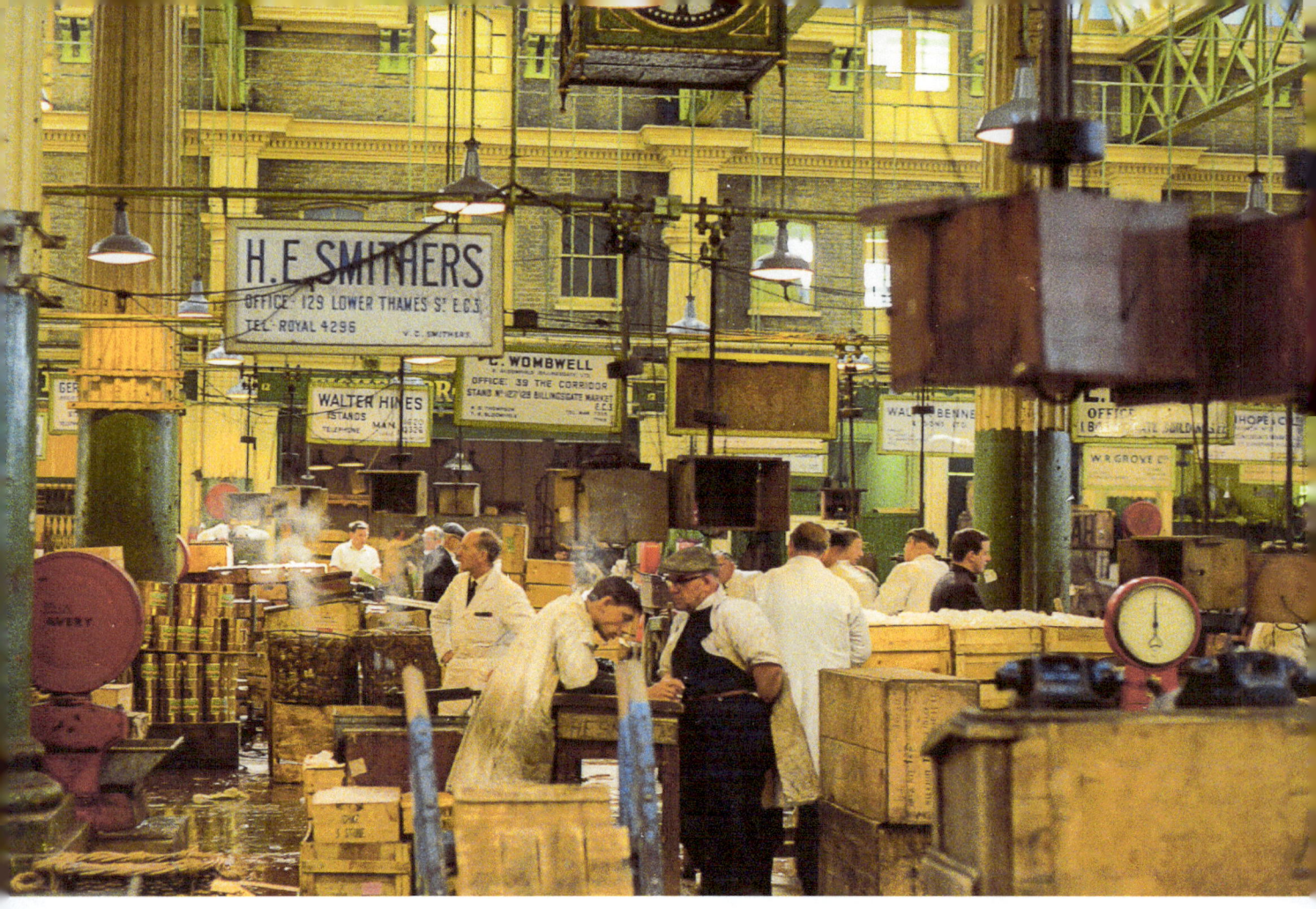

BILLINGGATE MARKET

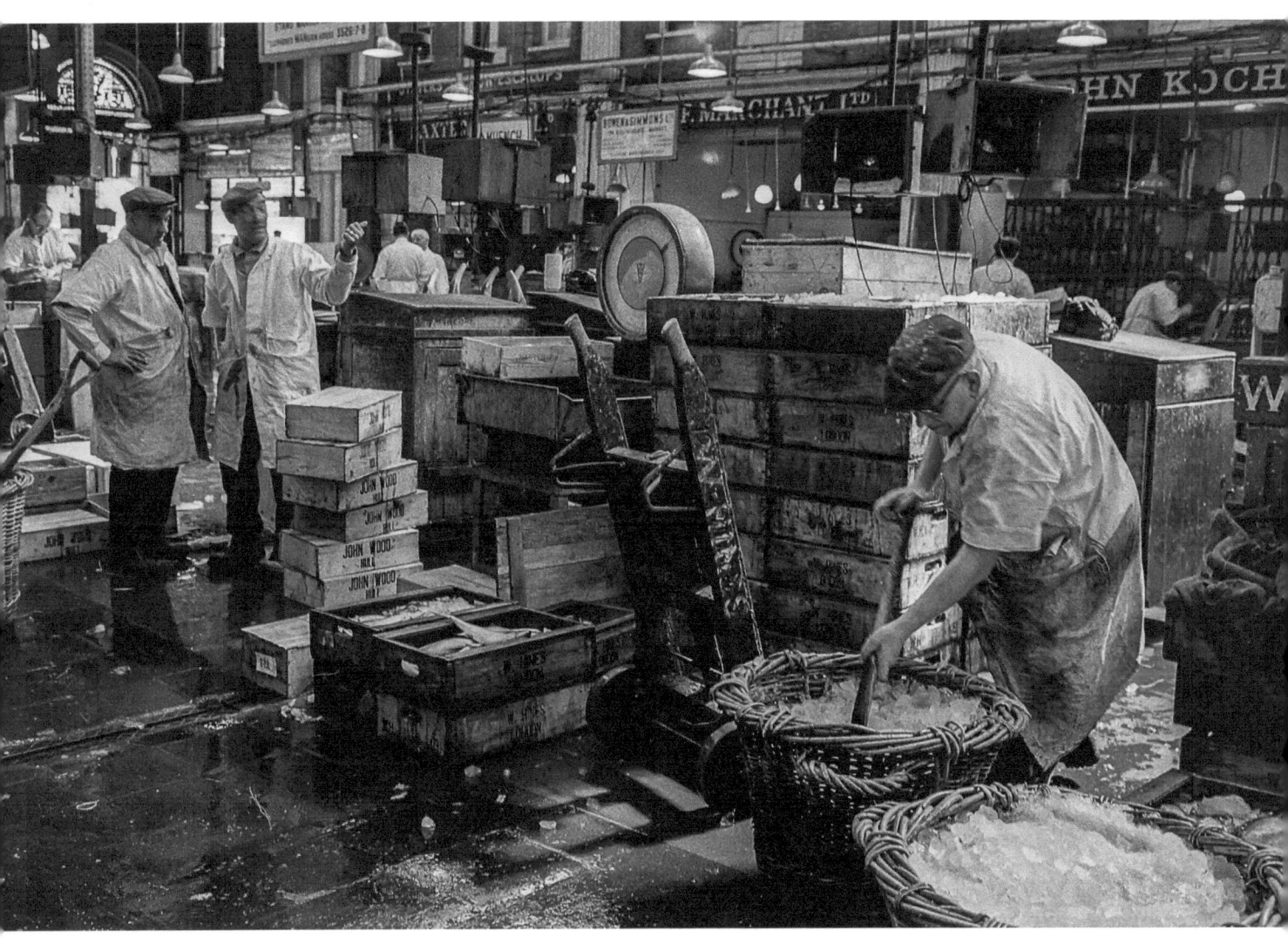

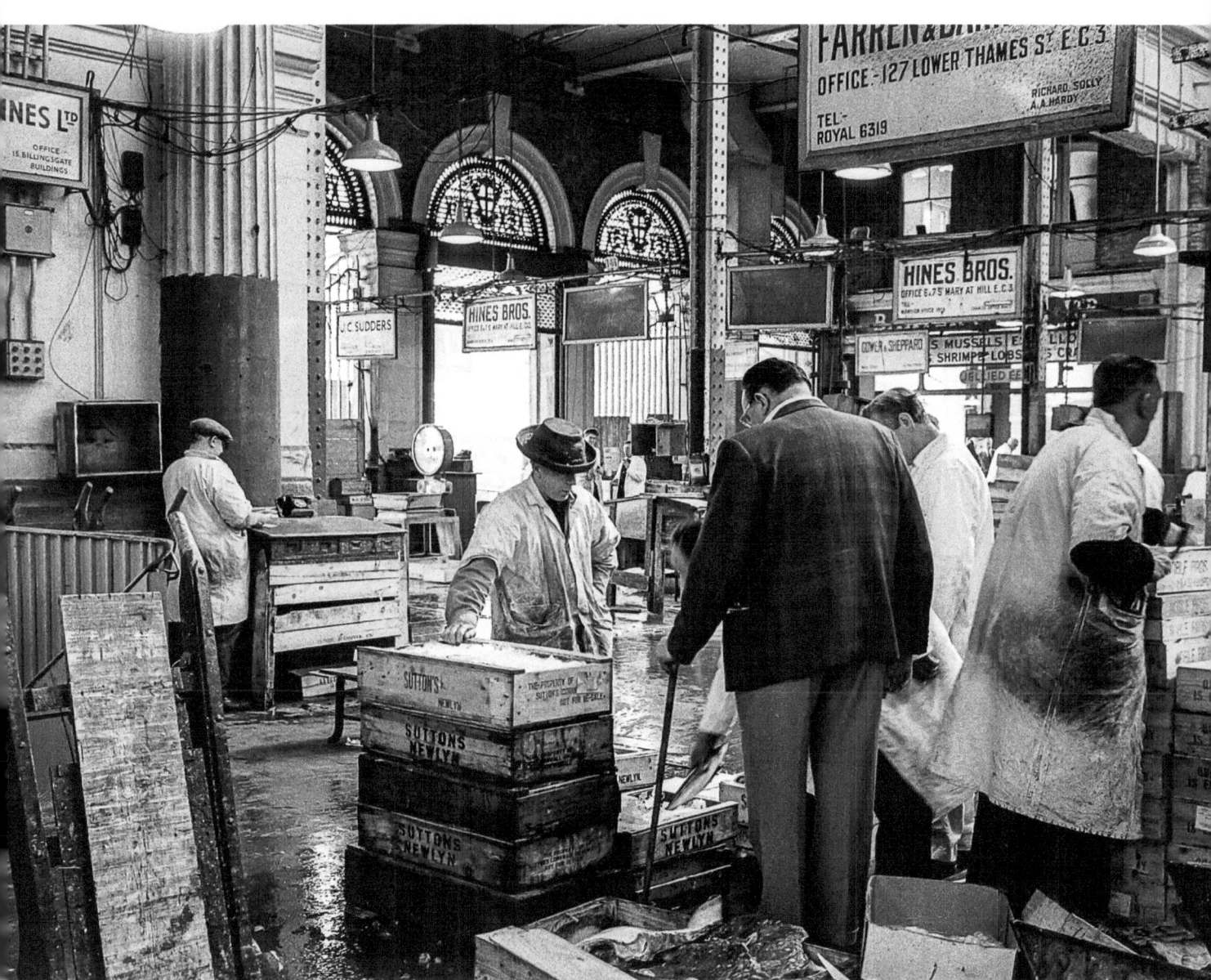

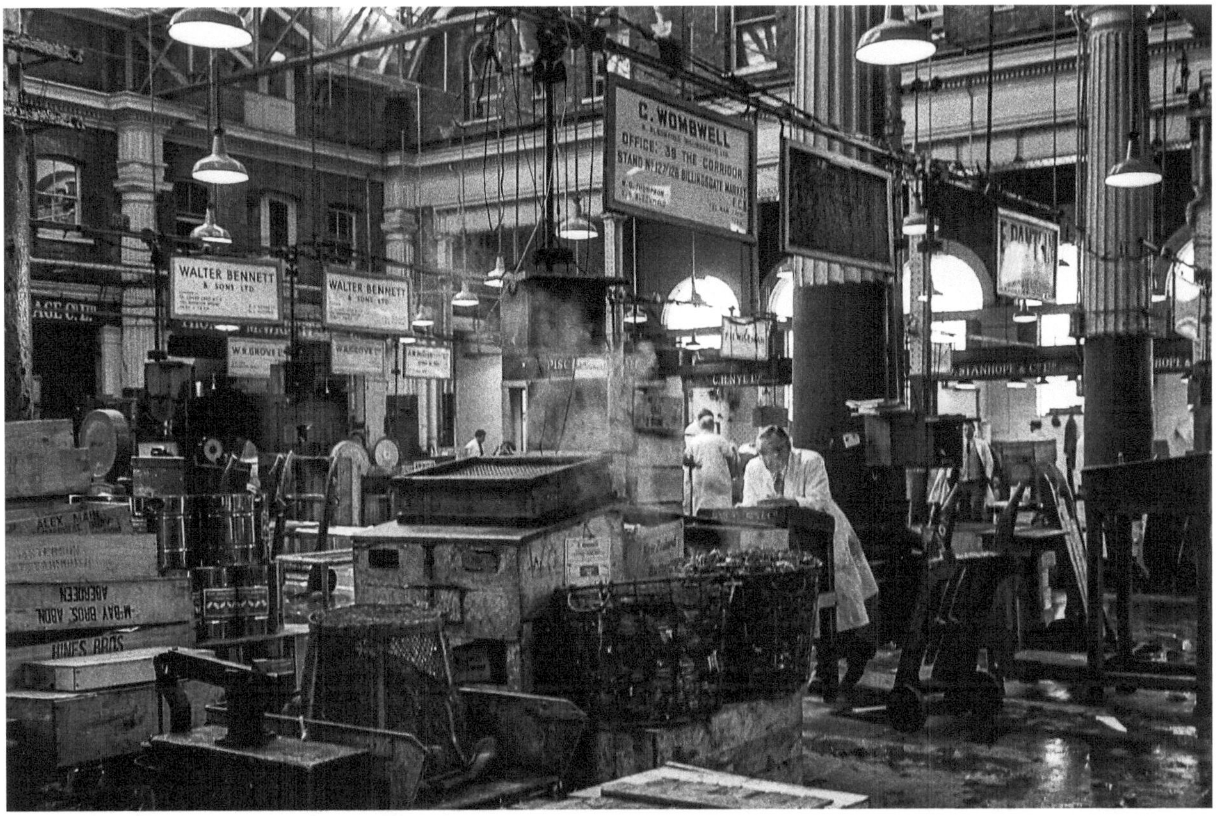

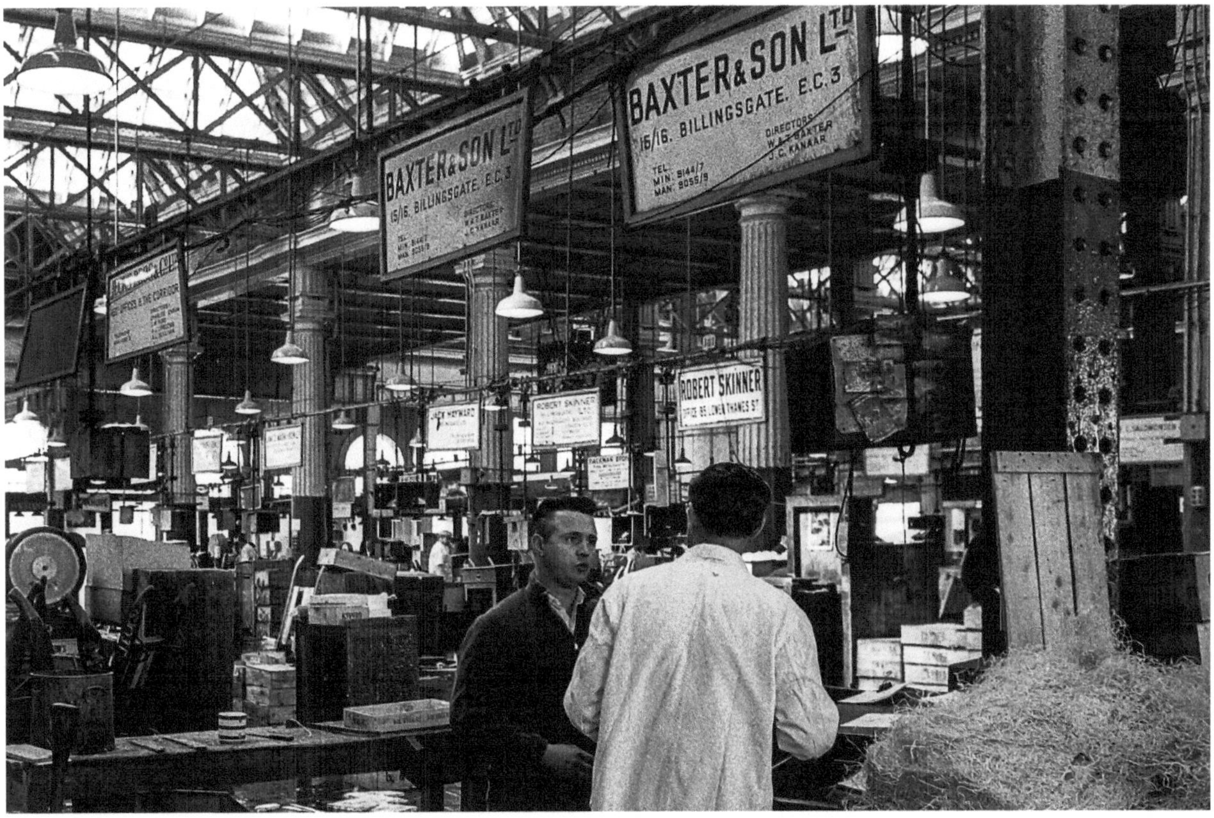

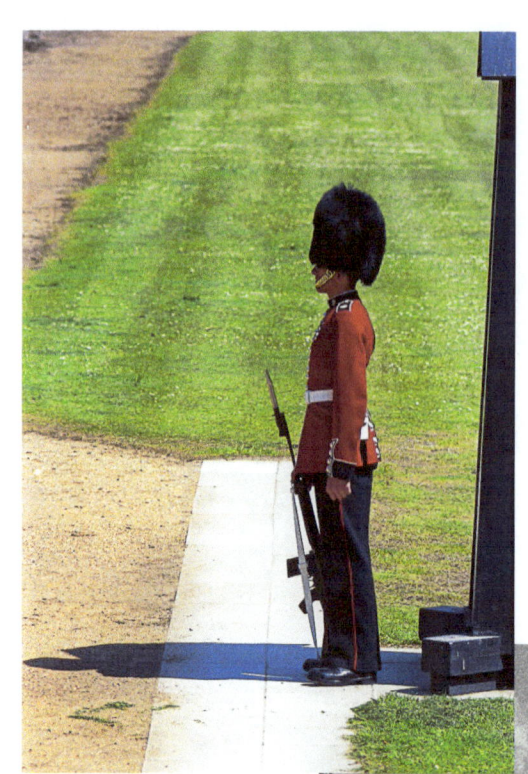

TOWER OF LONDON

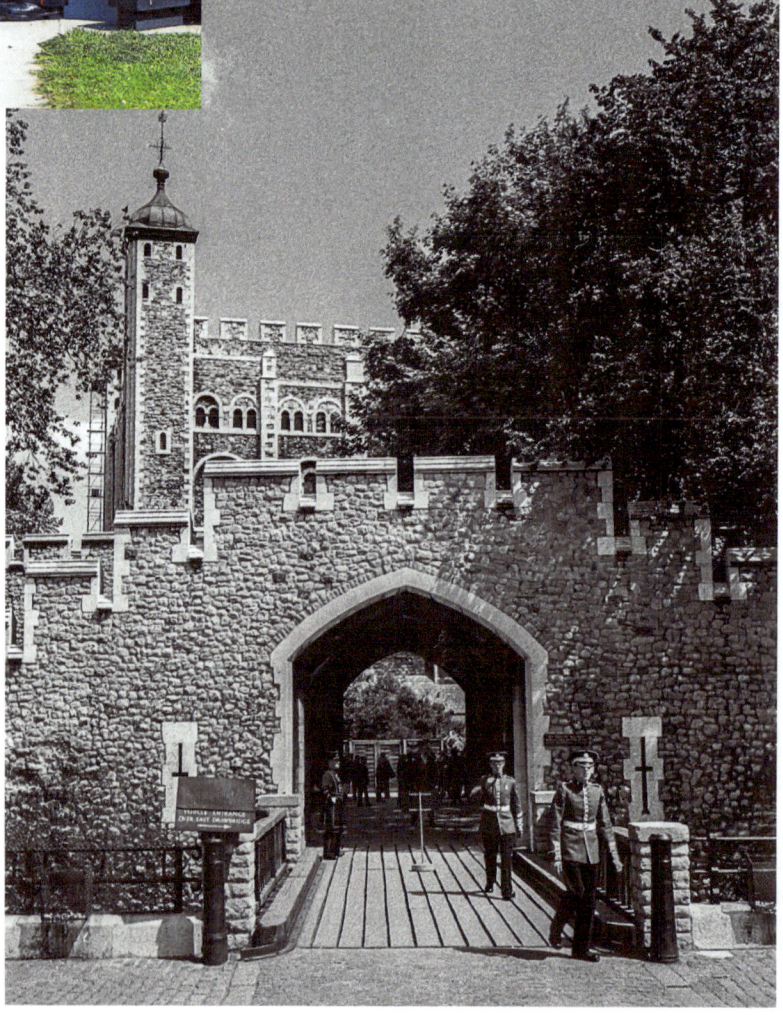

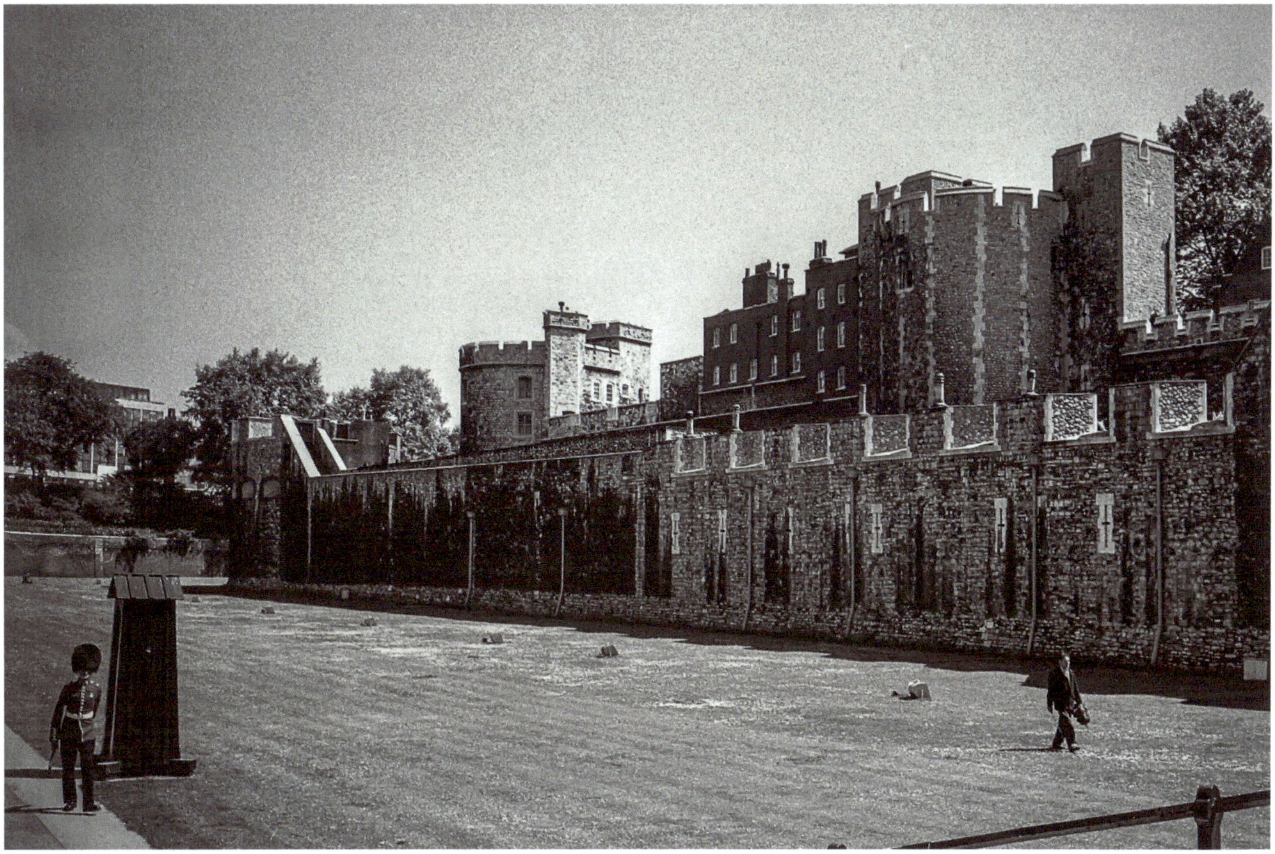

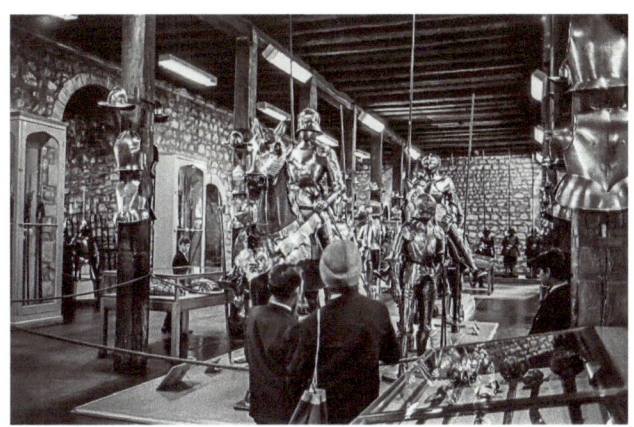
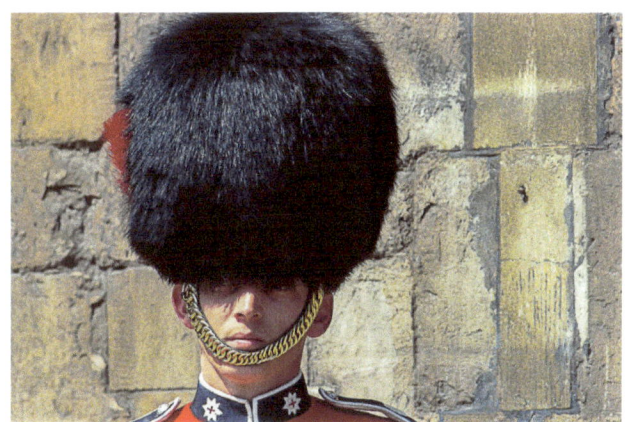

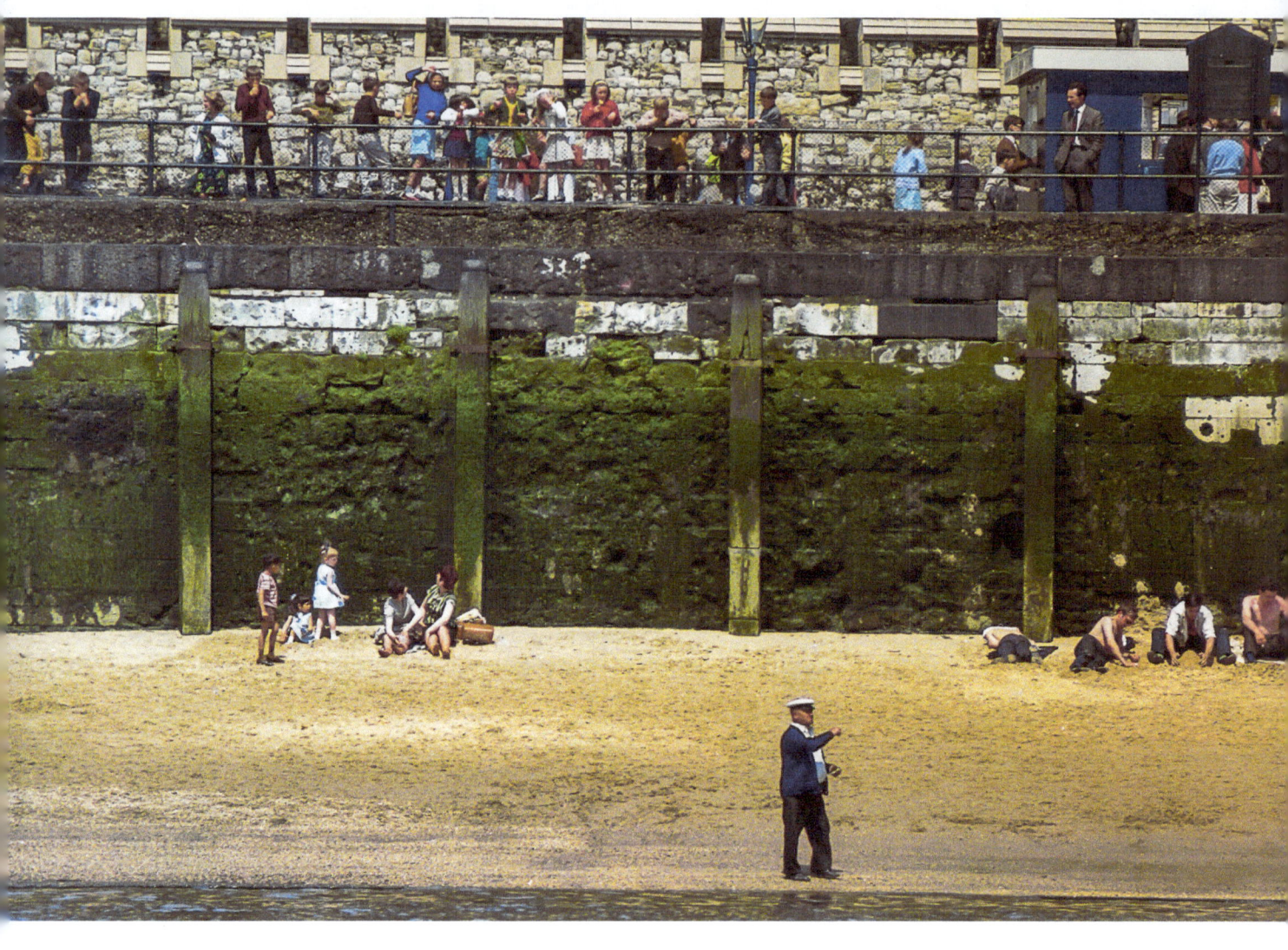

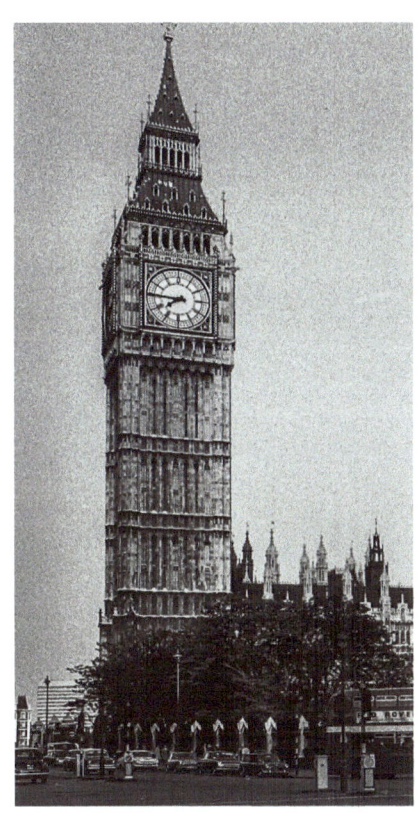
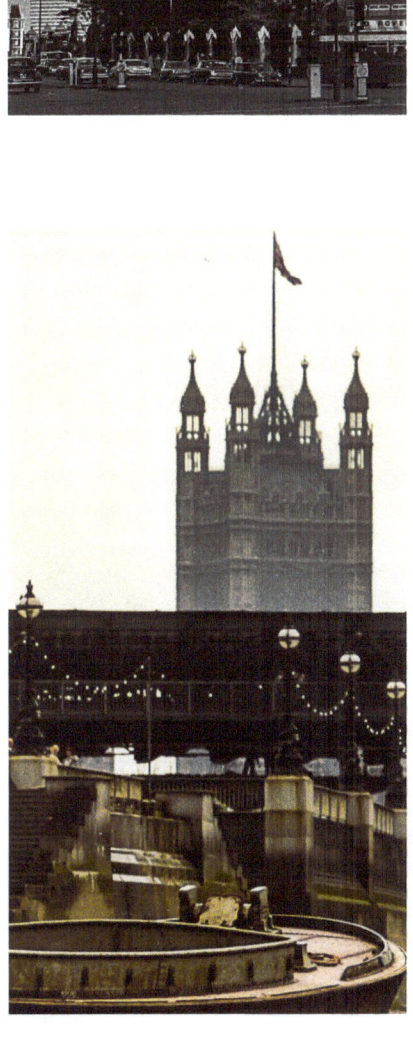

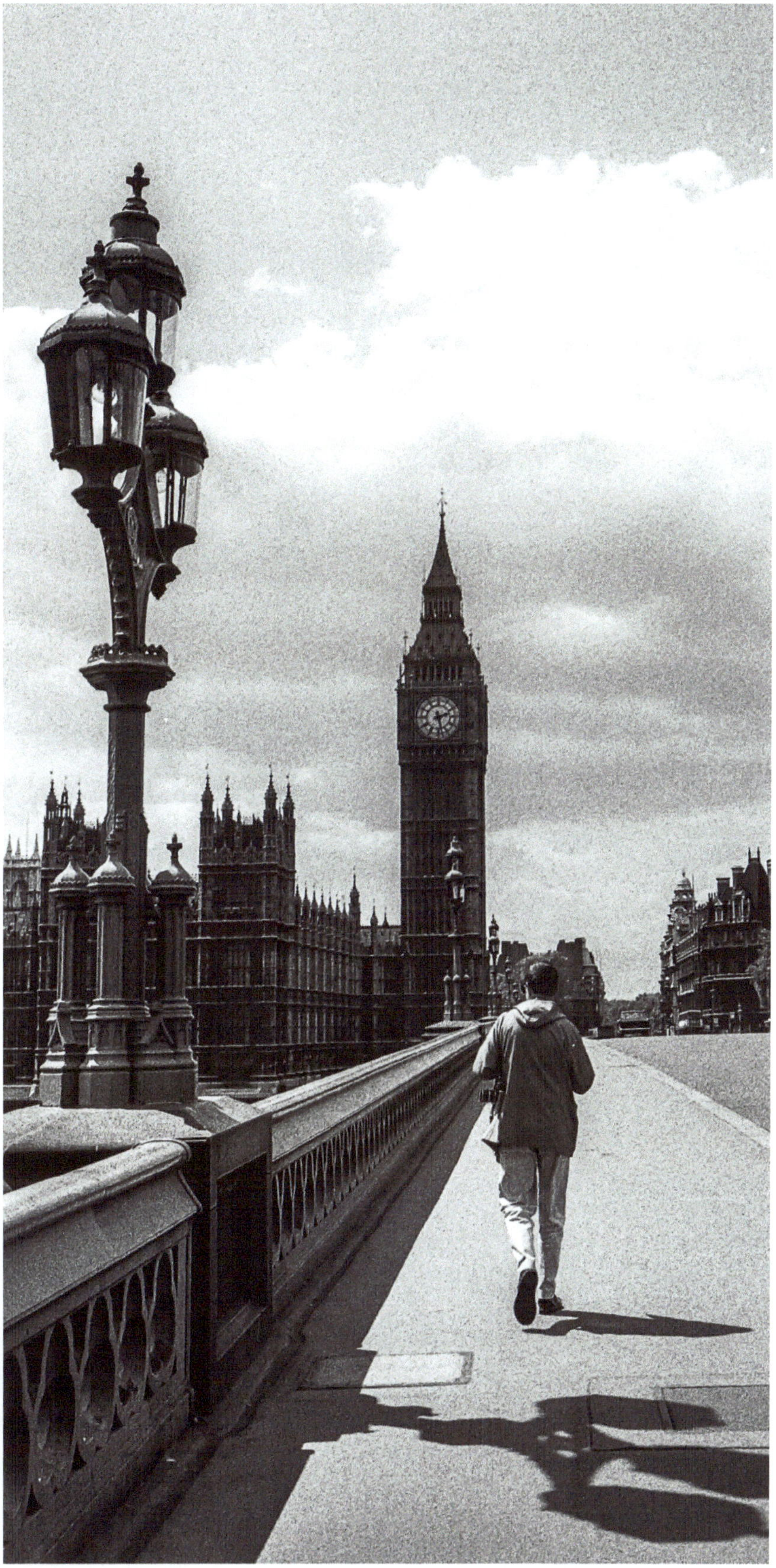

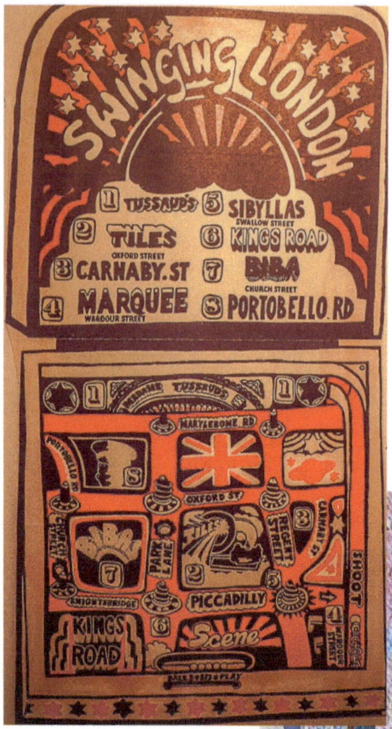

CARNABY STREET

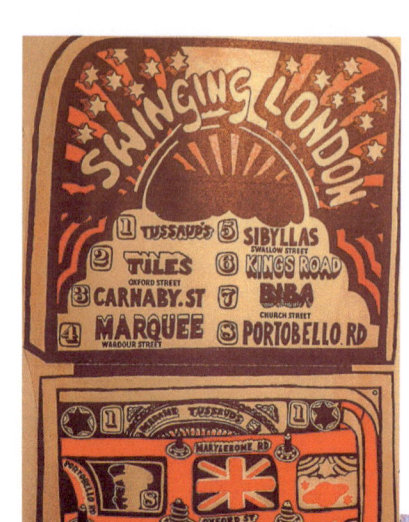

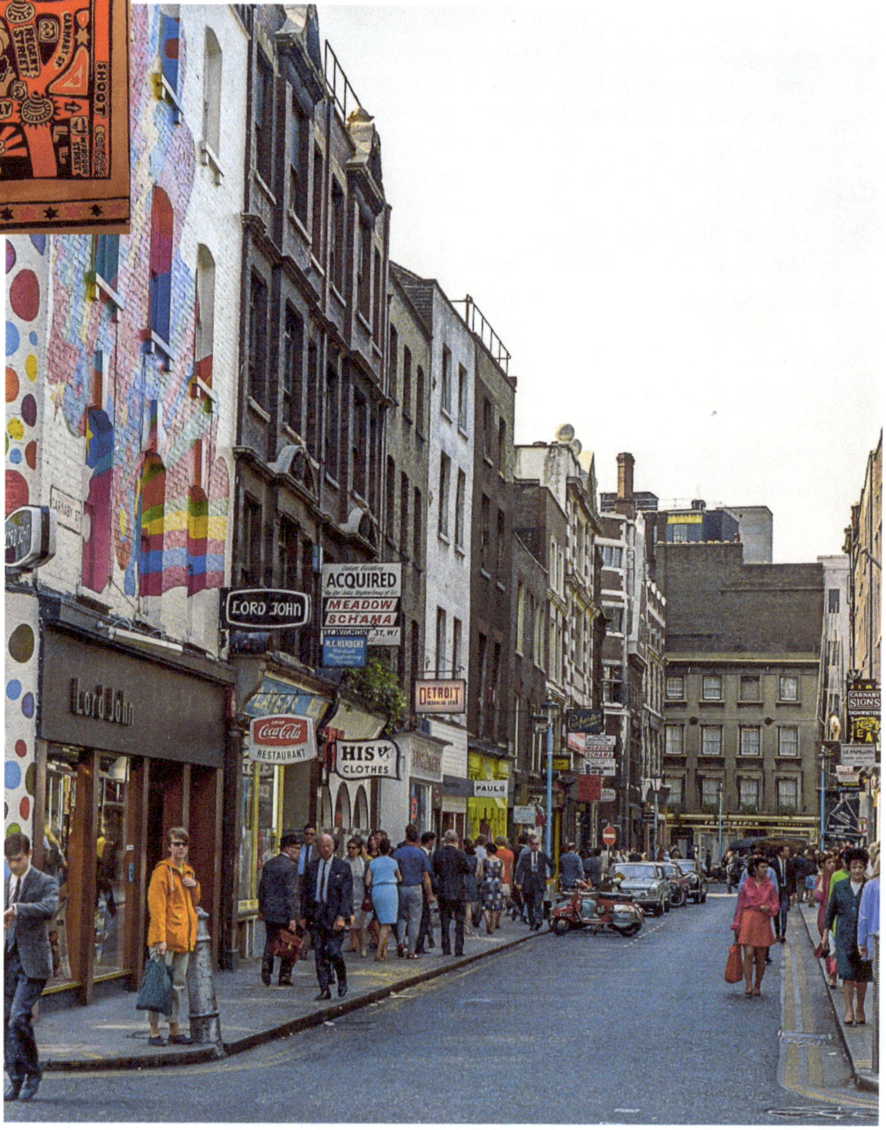

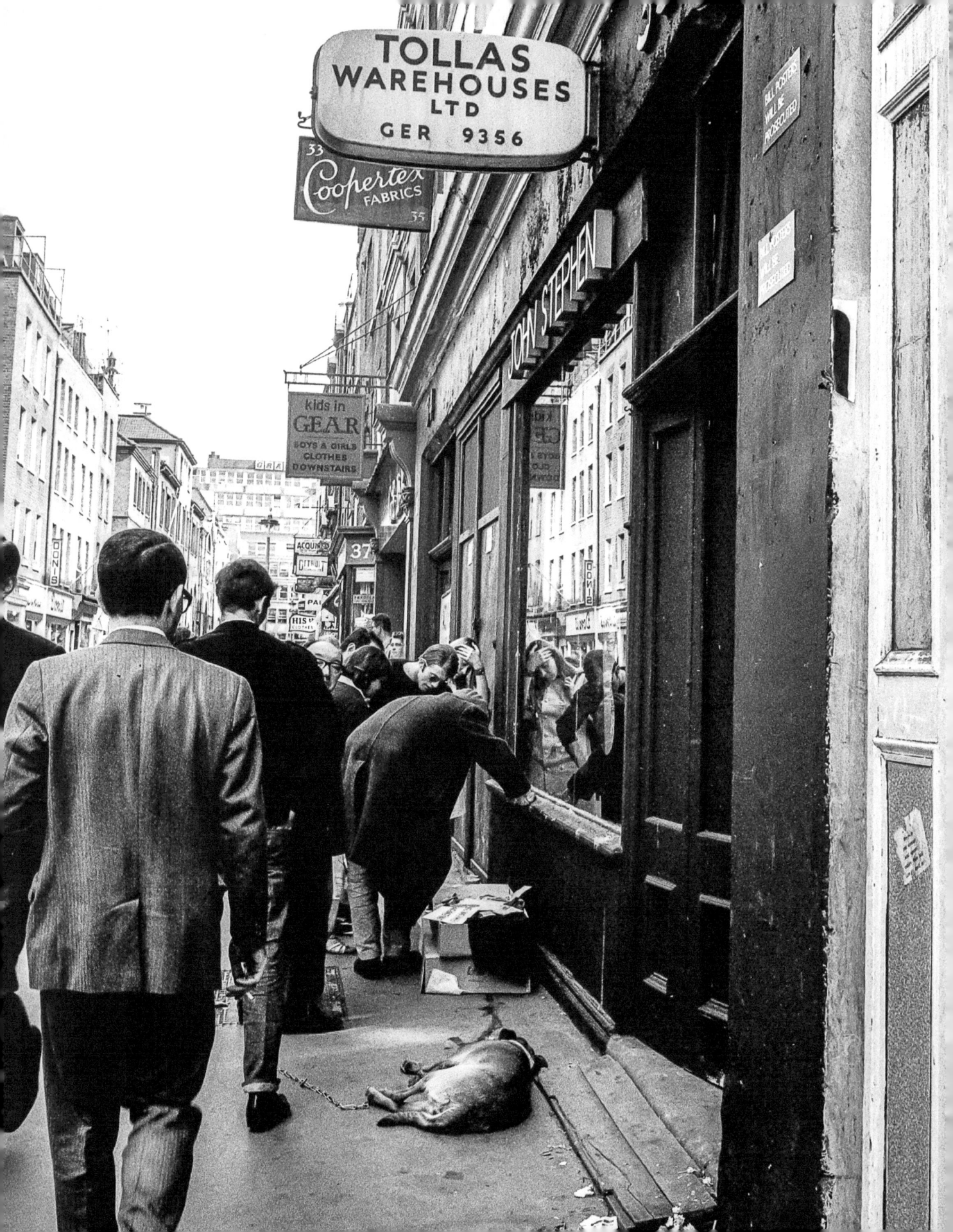

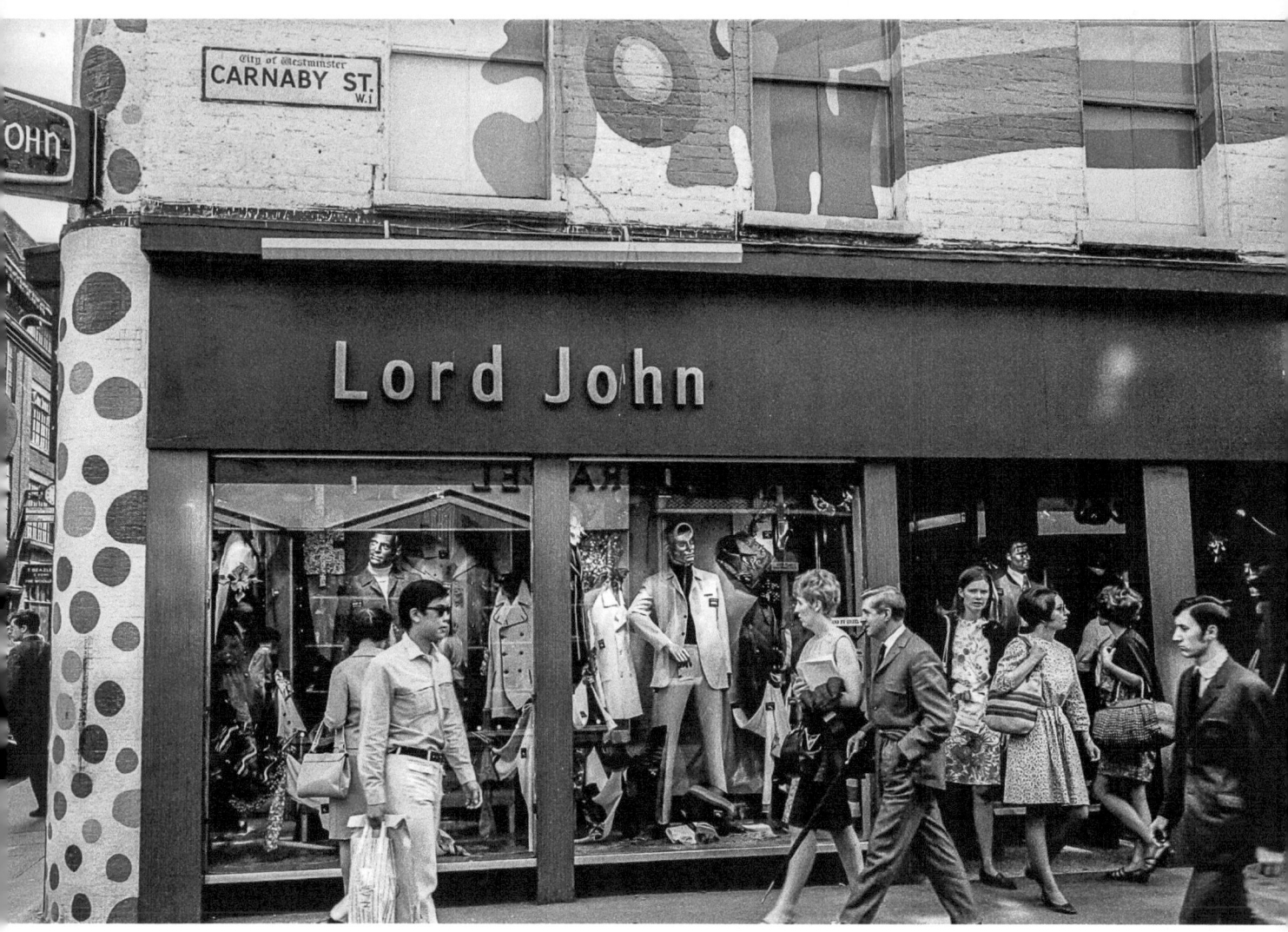

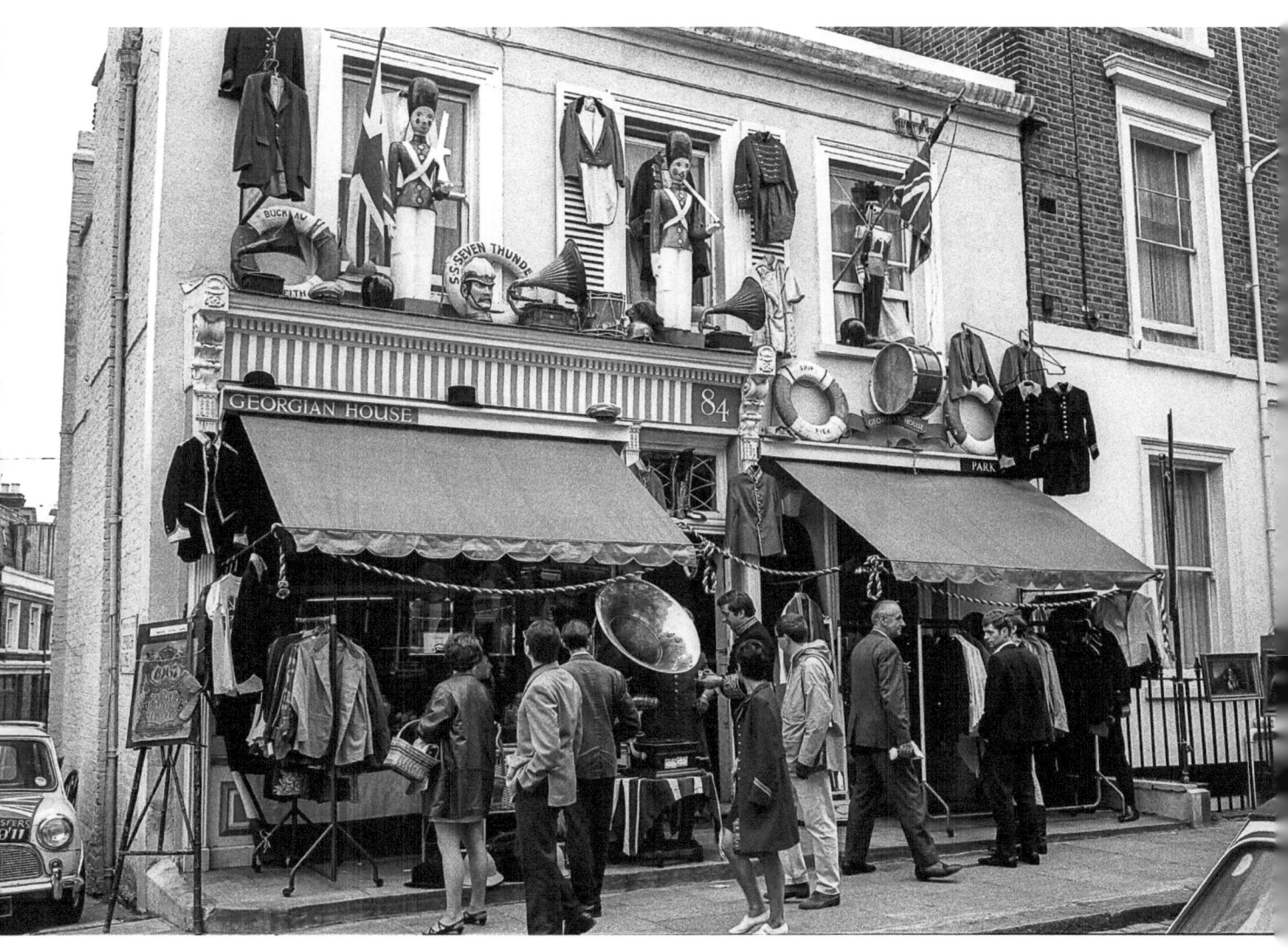

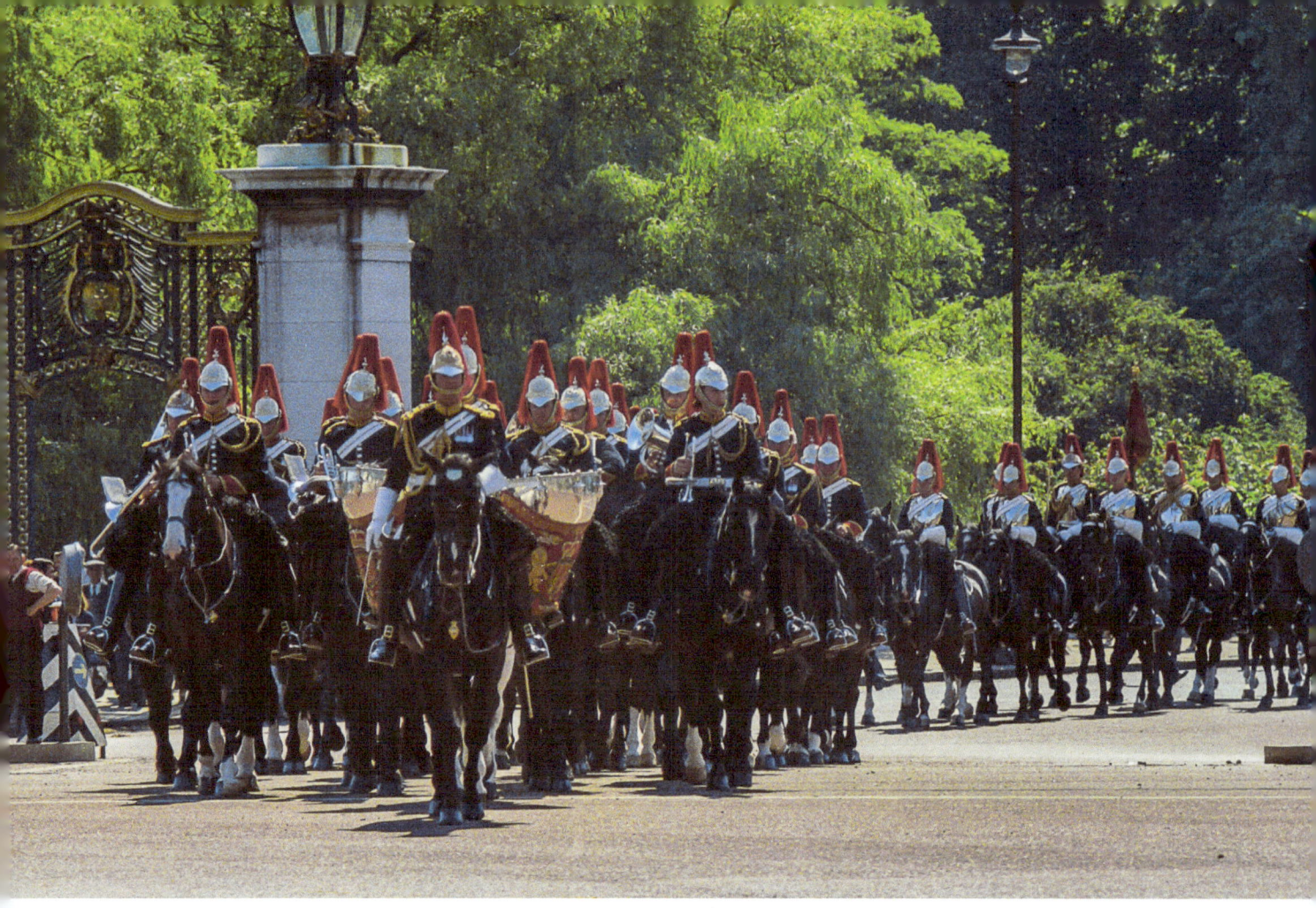

CHANGING THE GUARD

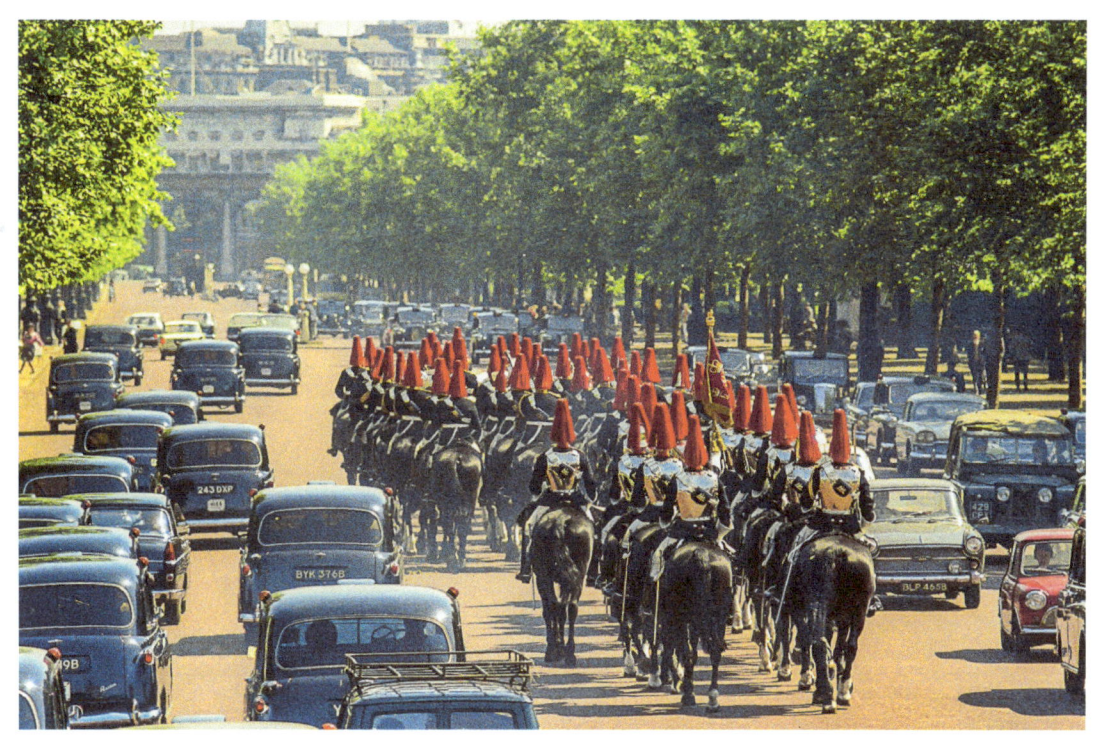
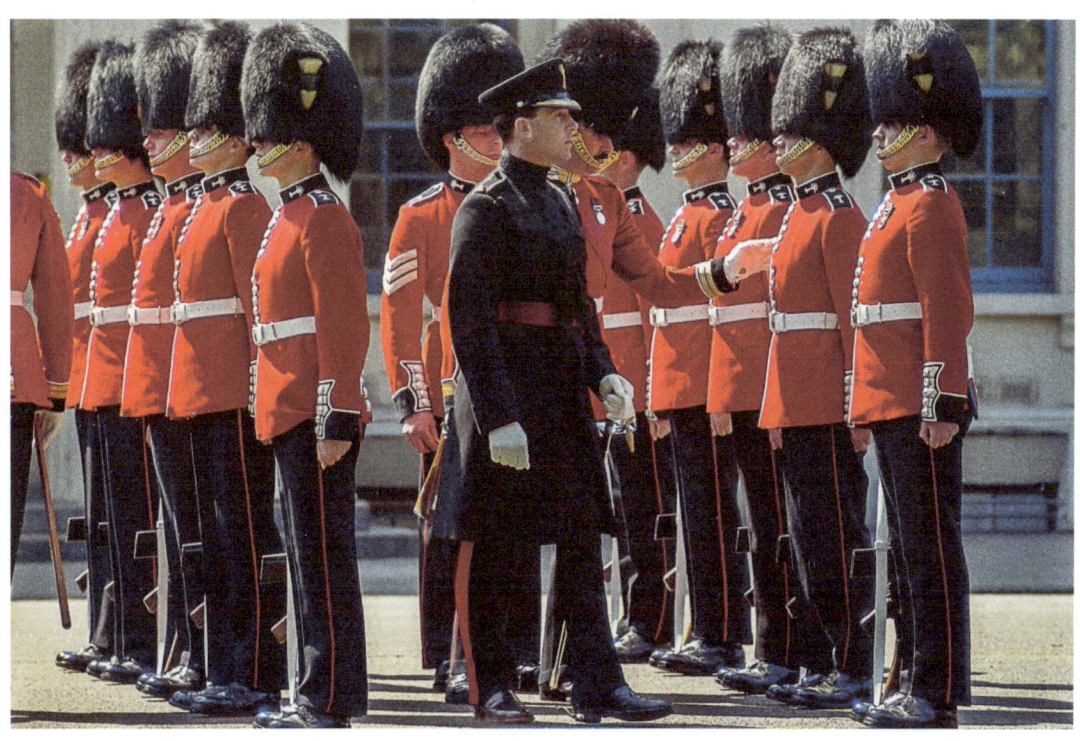

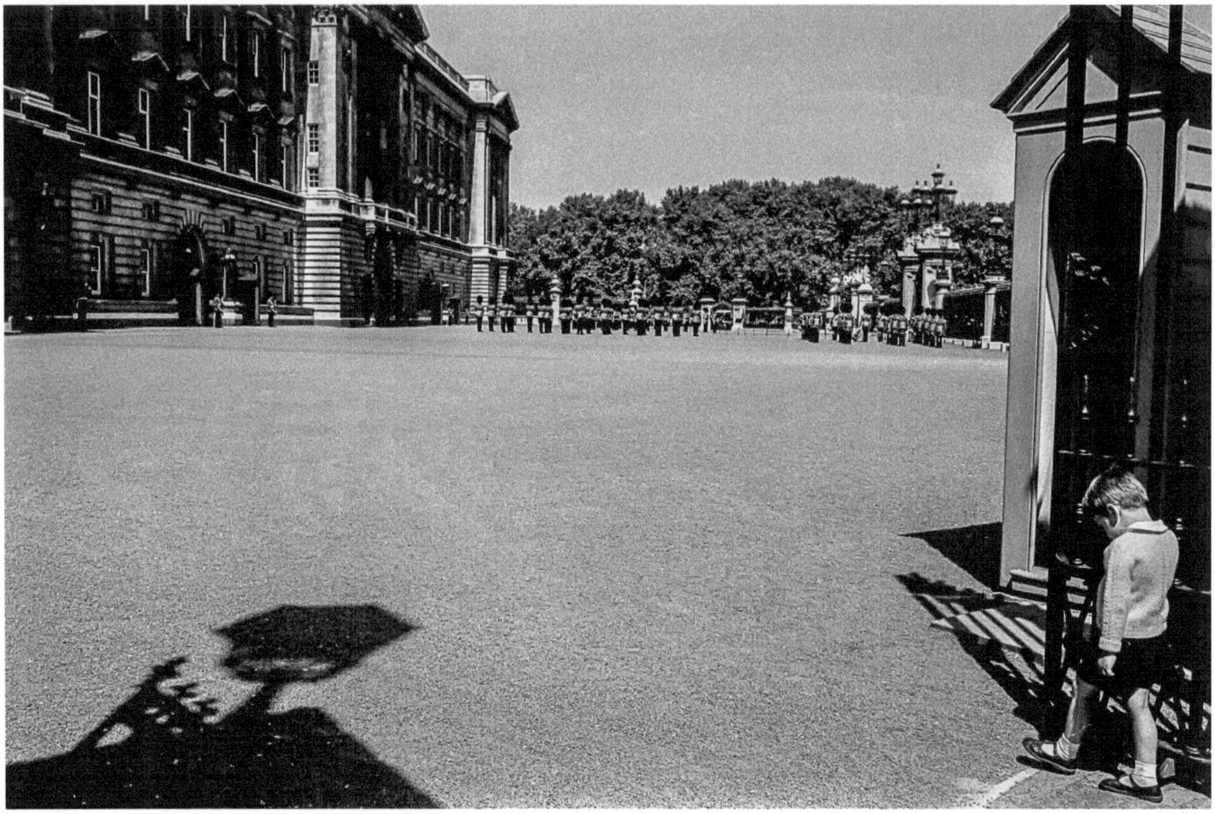

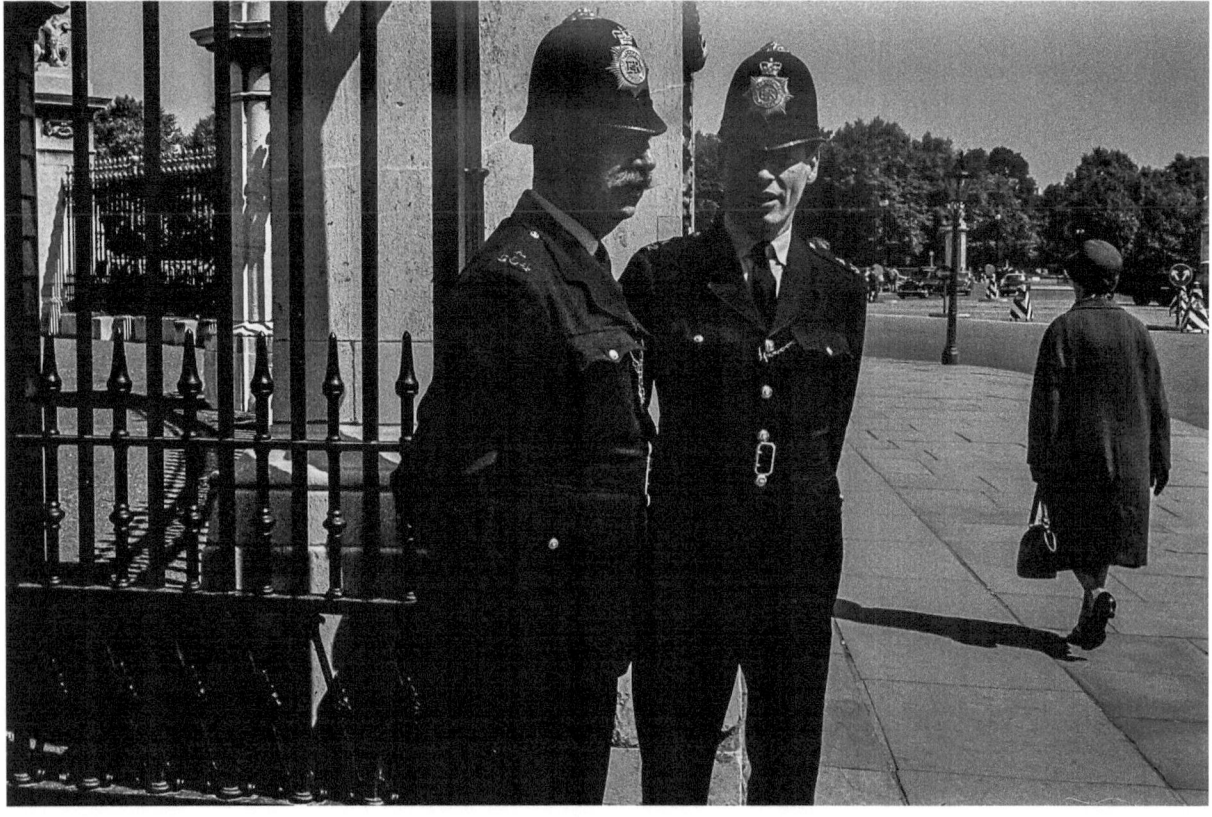

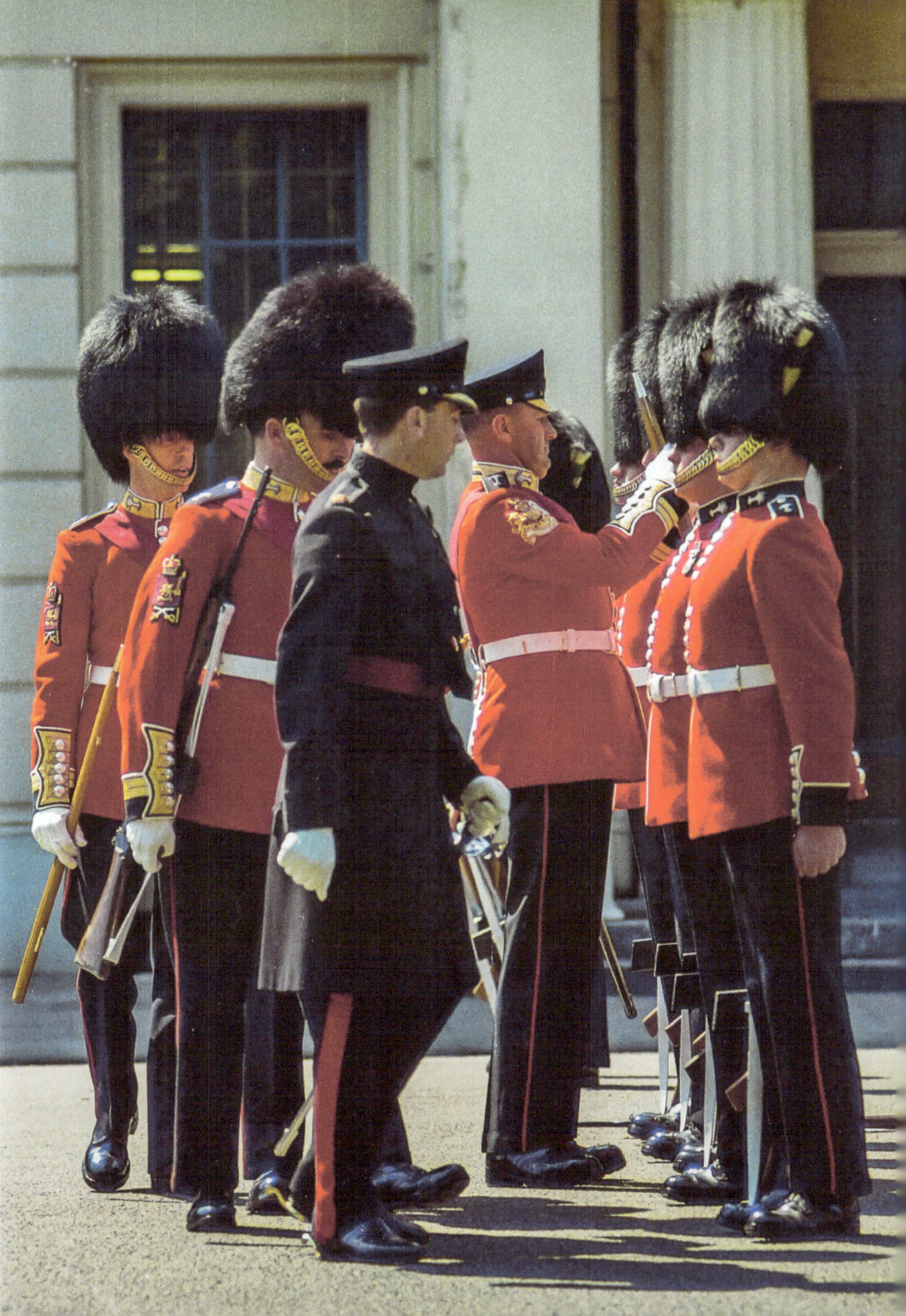

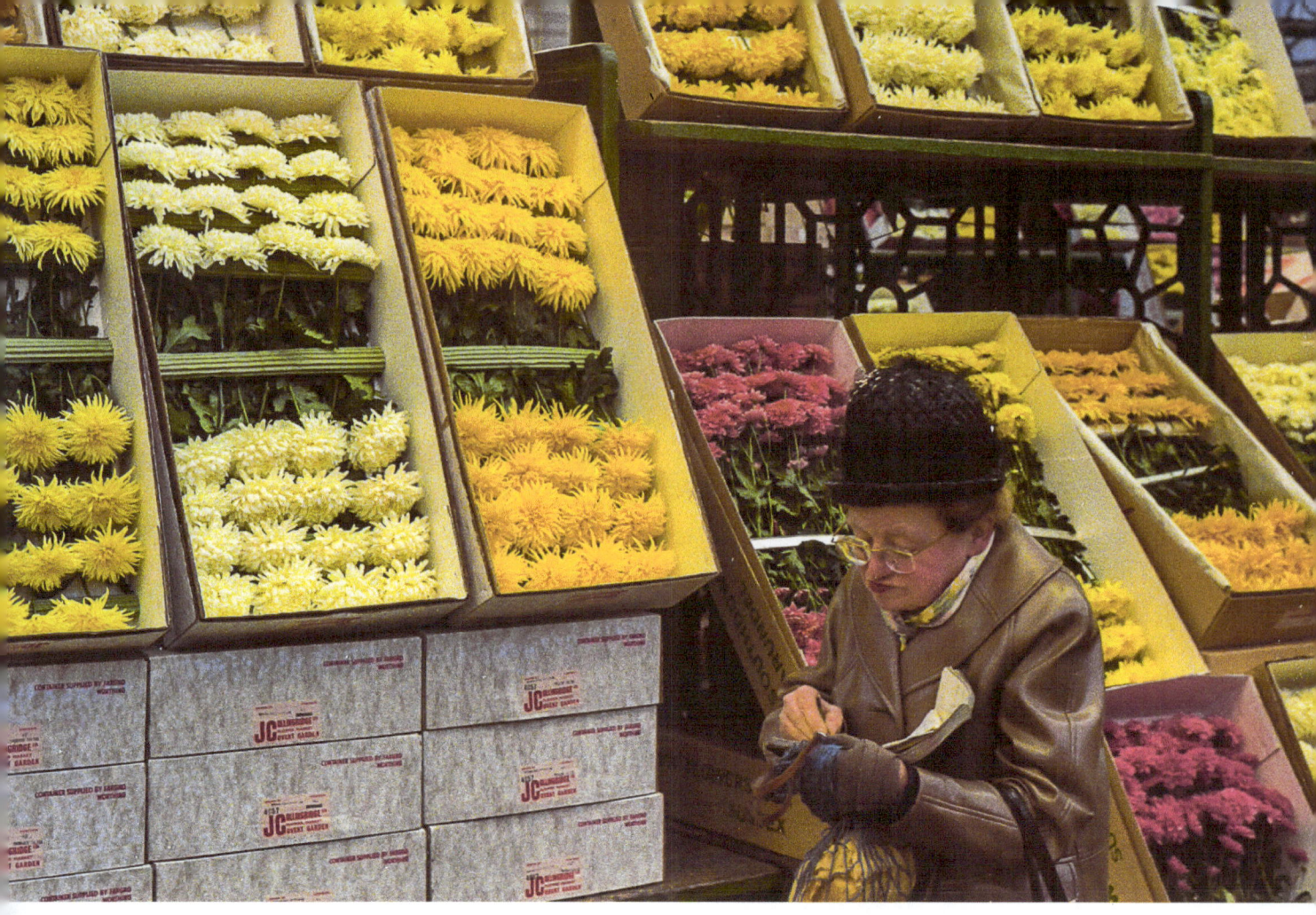

COVENT GARDEN

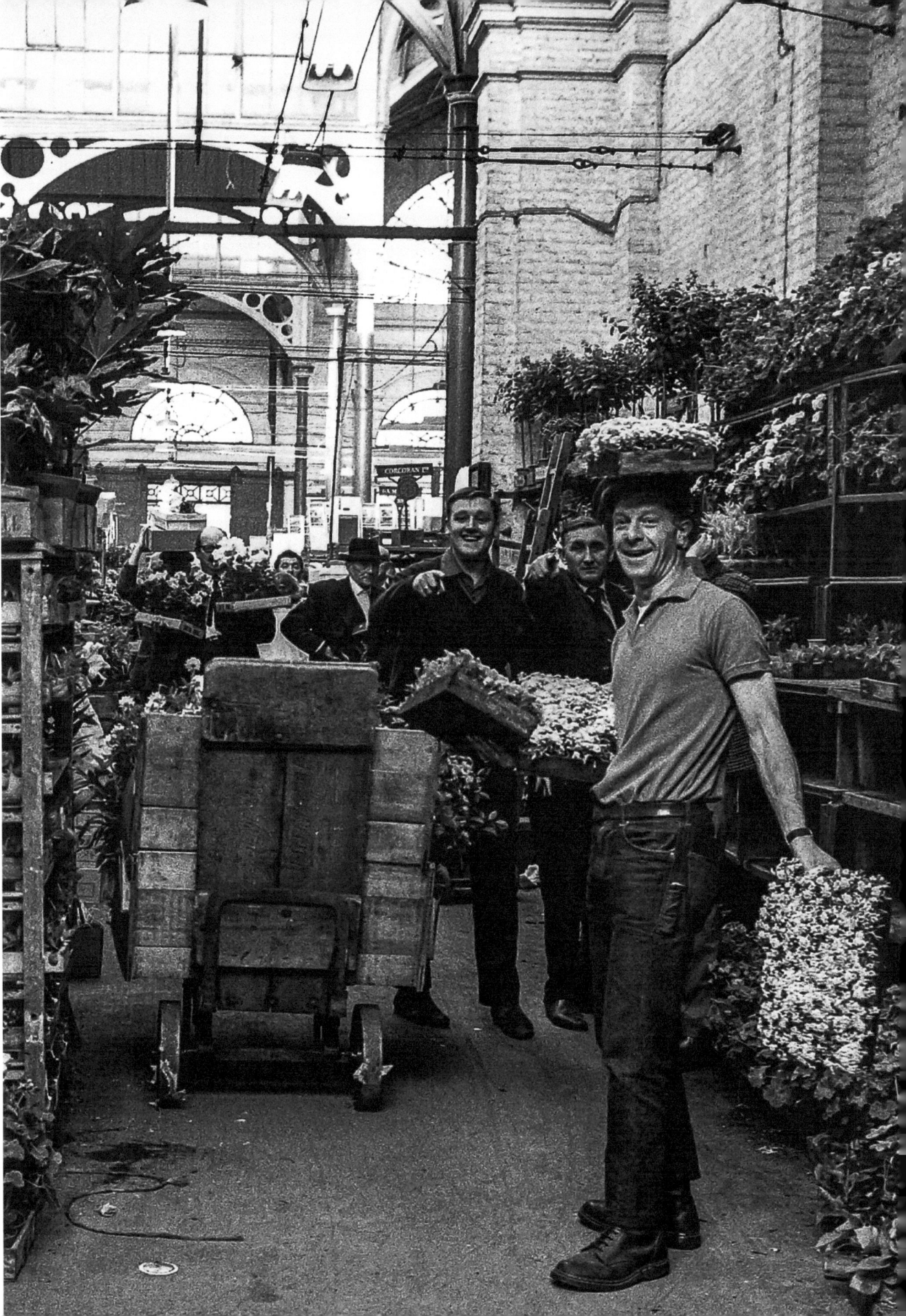

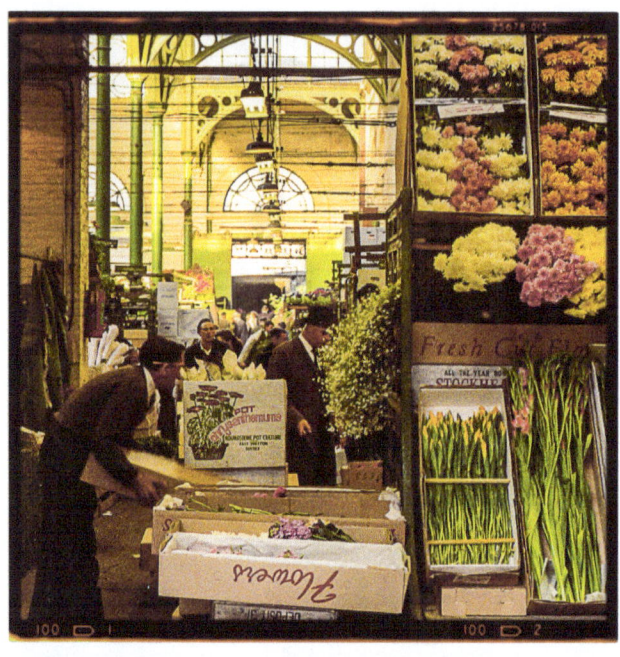
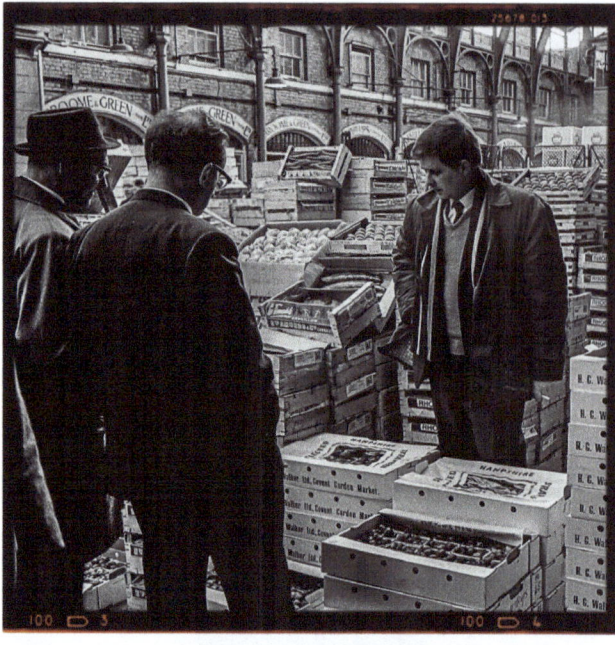
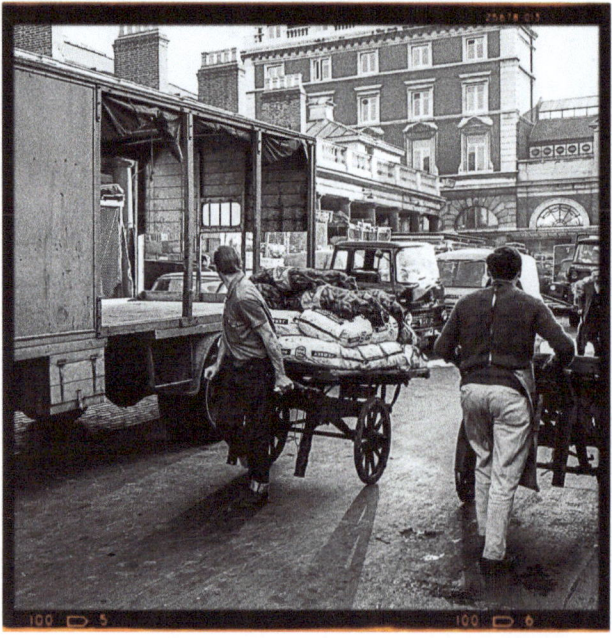
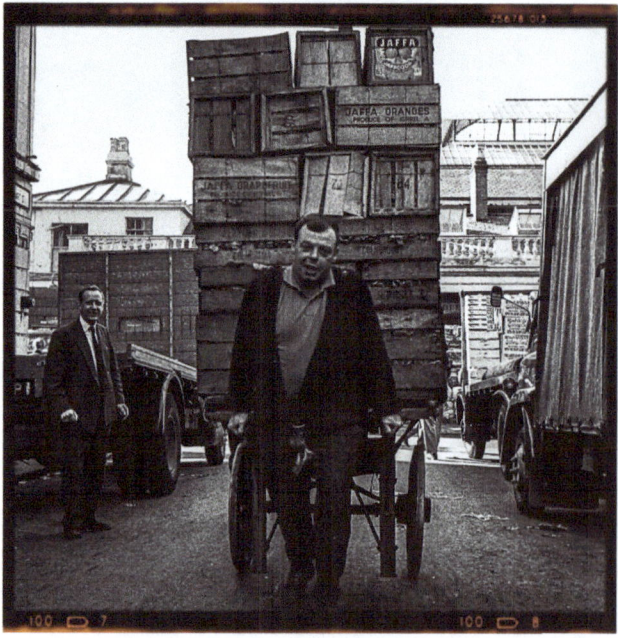

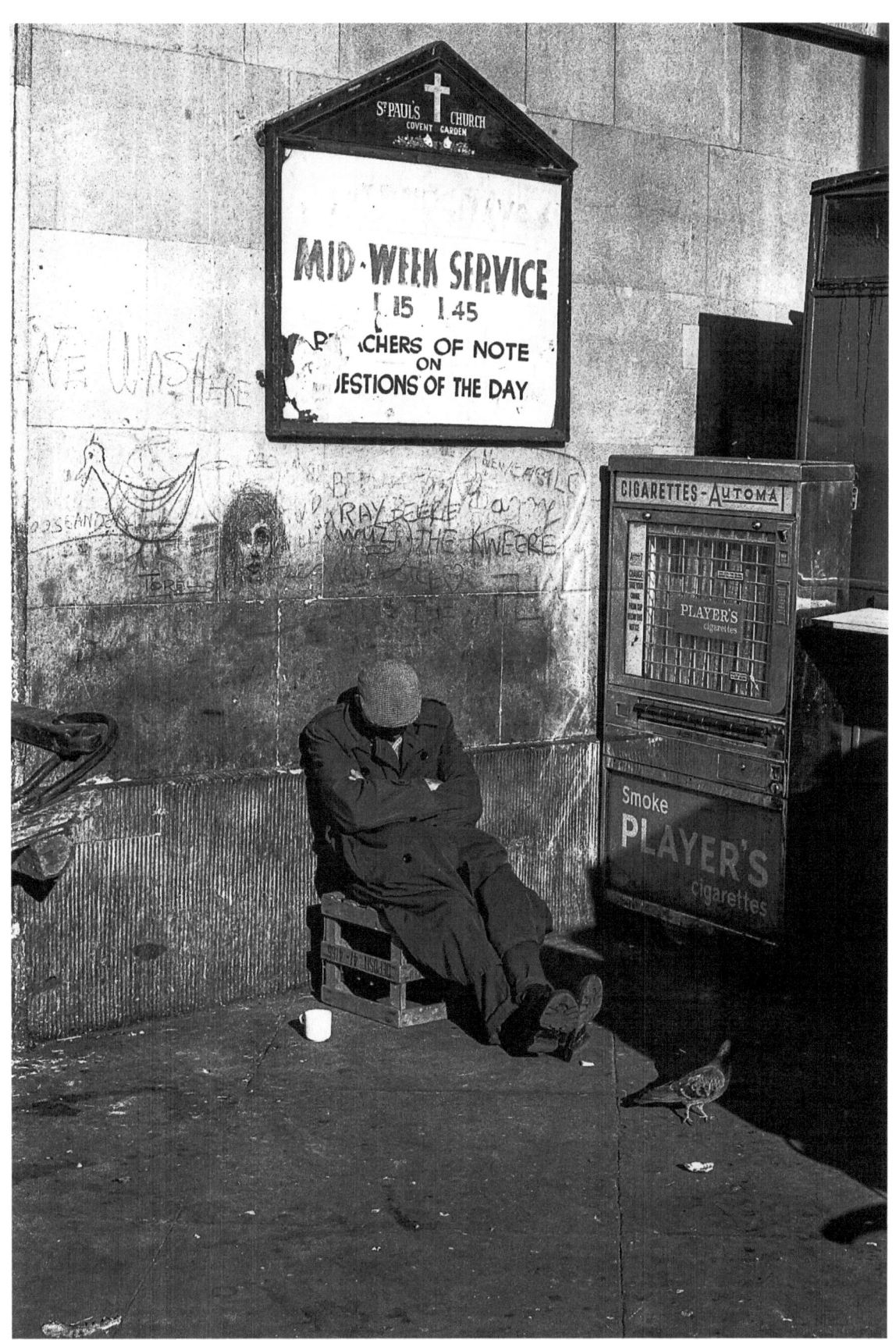

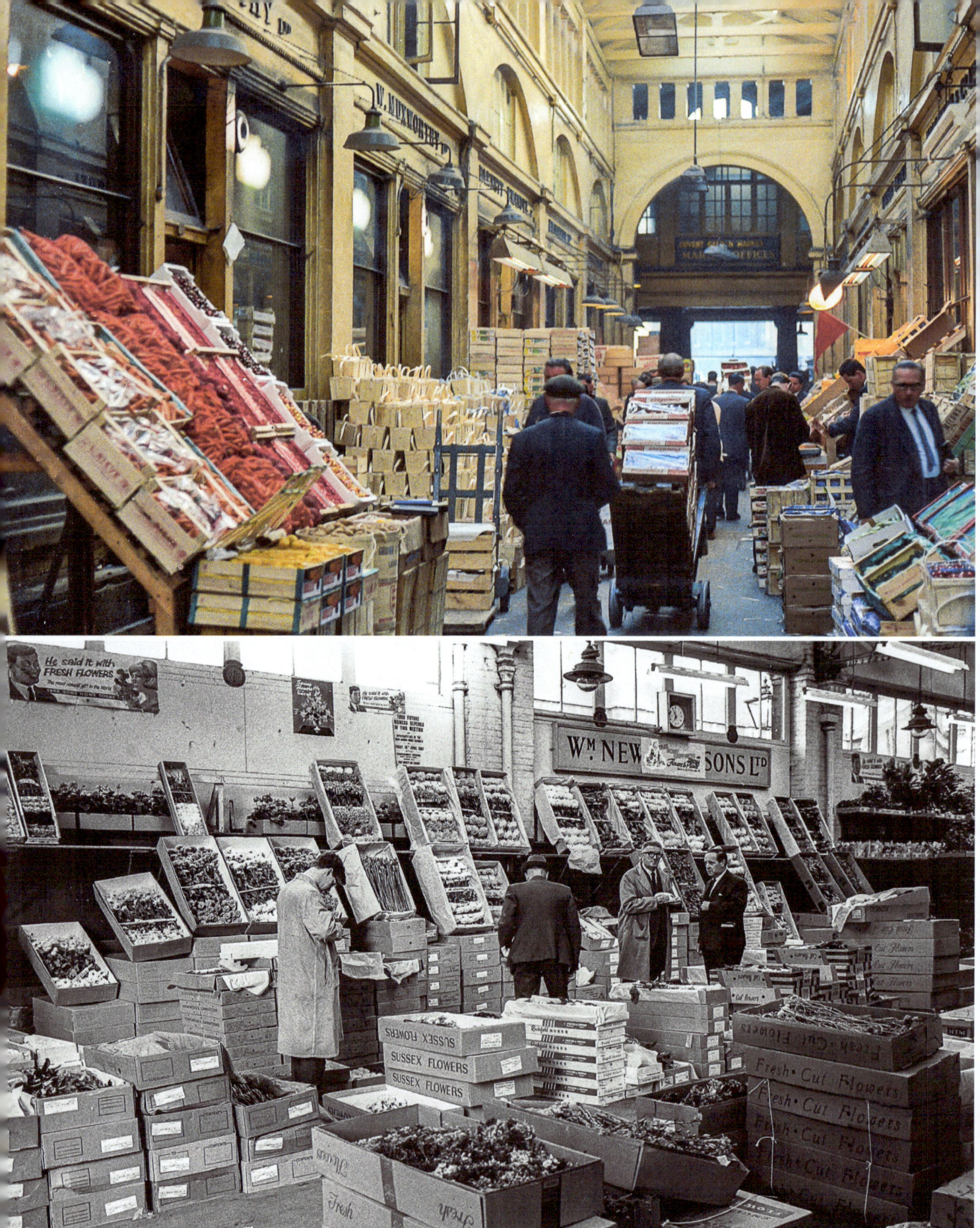

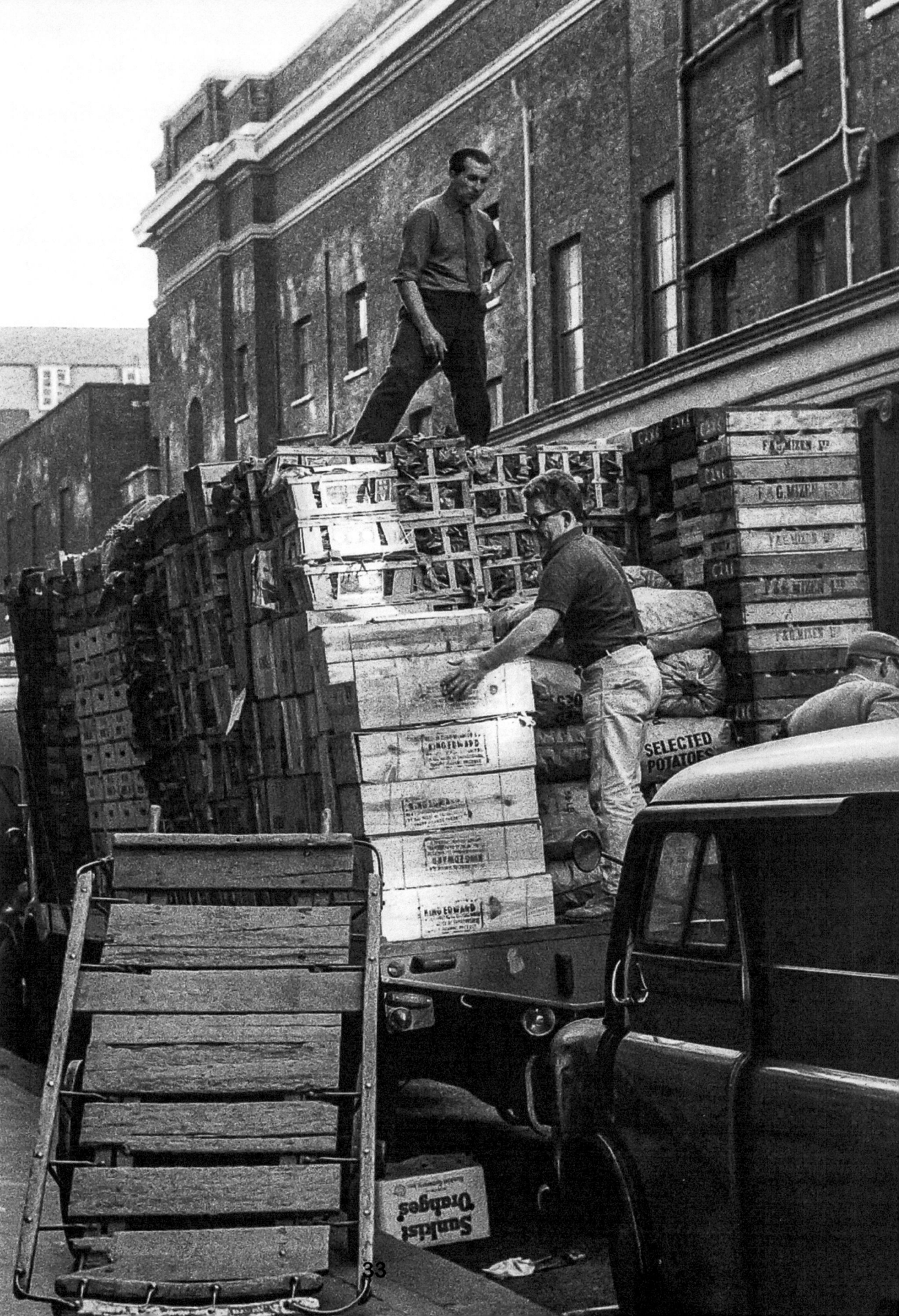

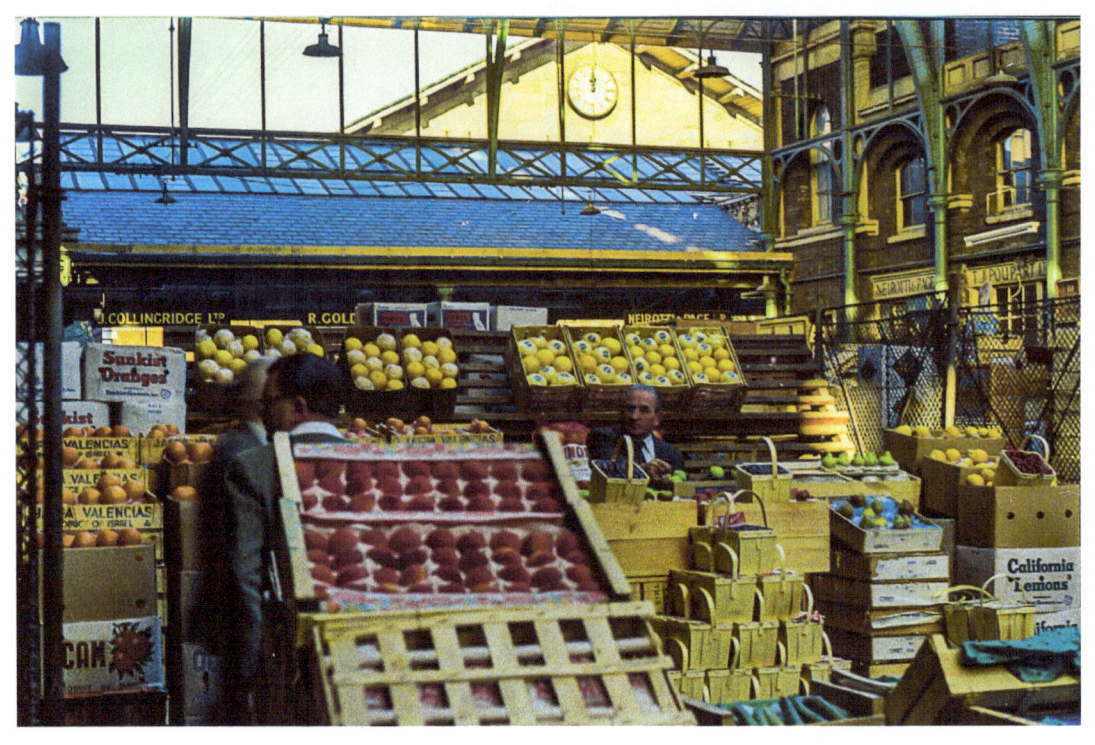

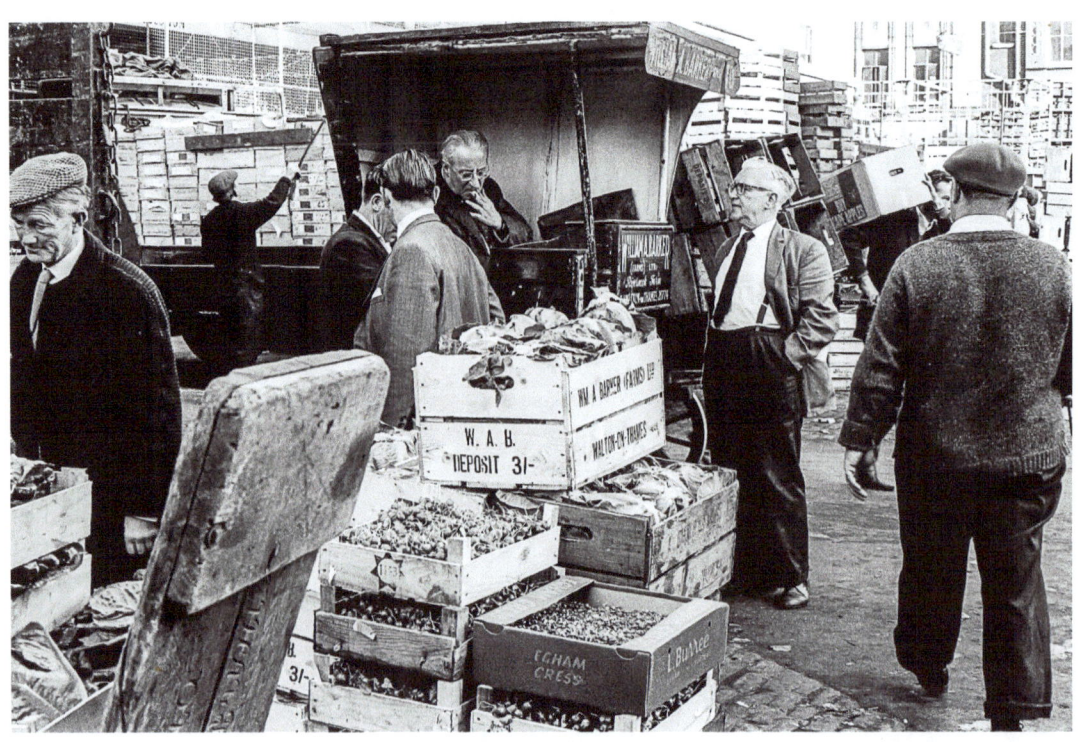

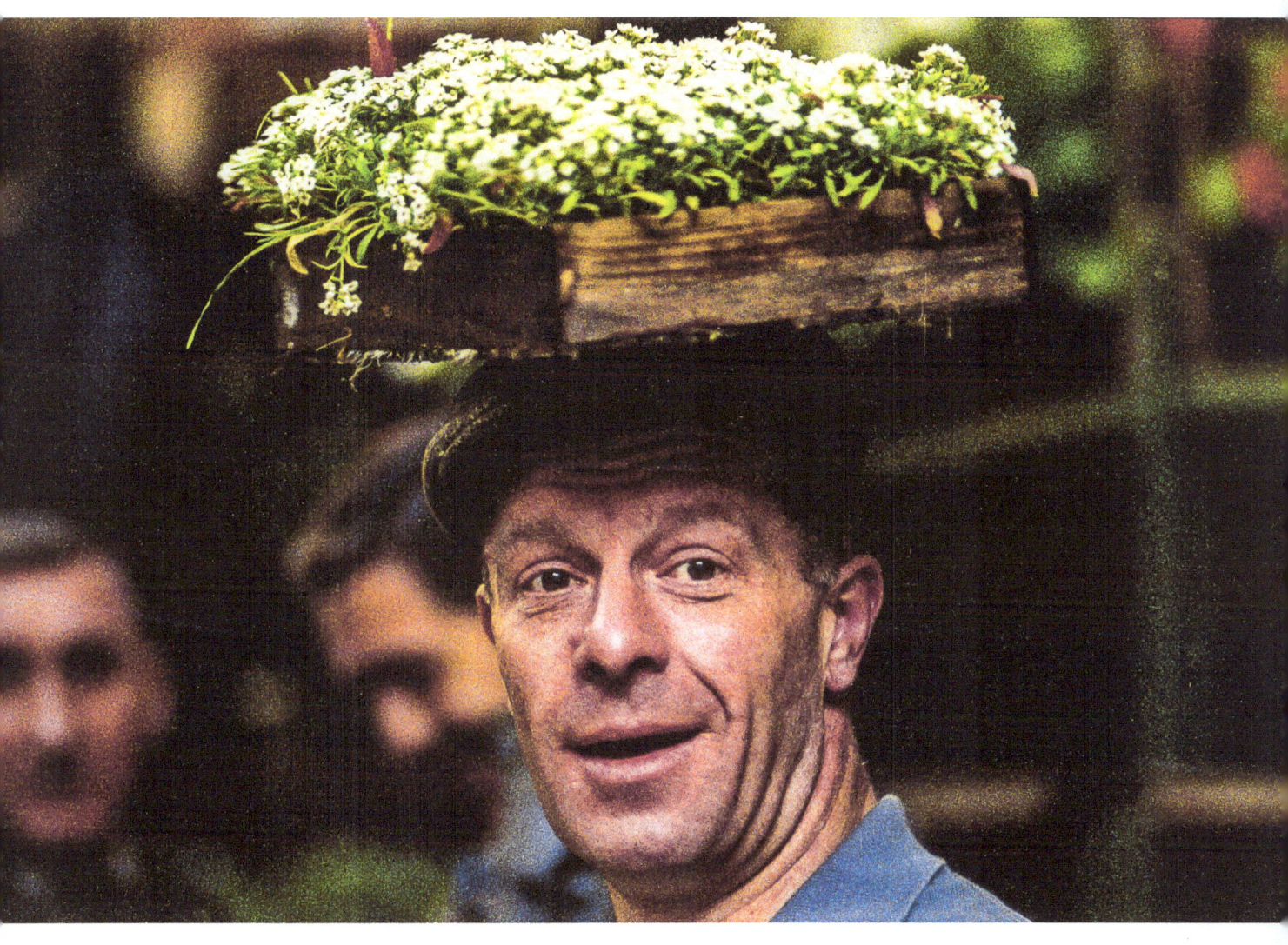

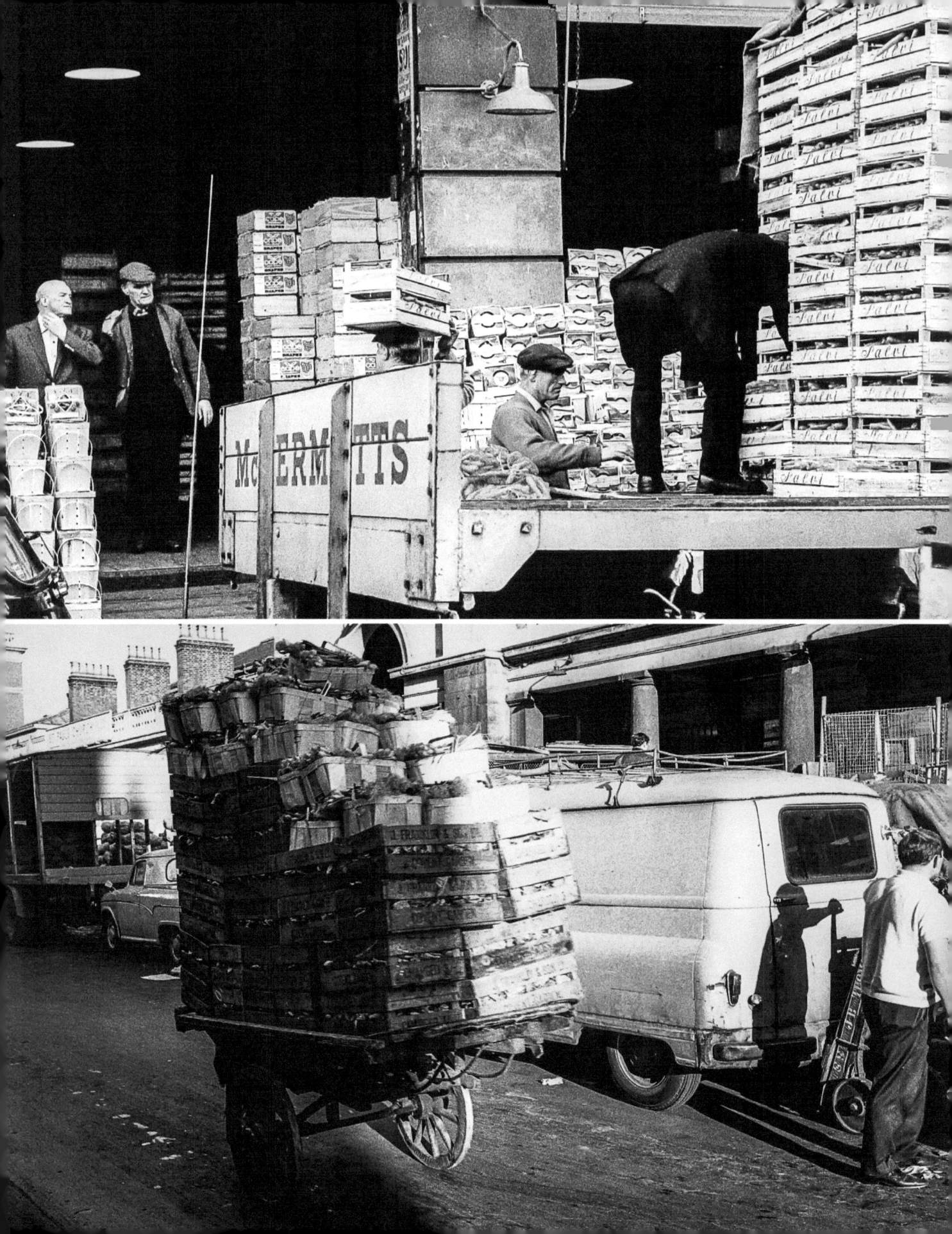

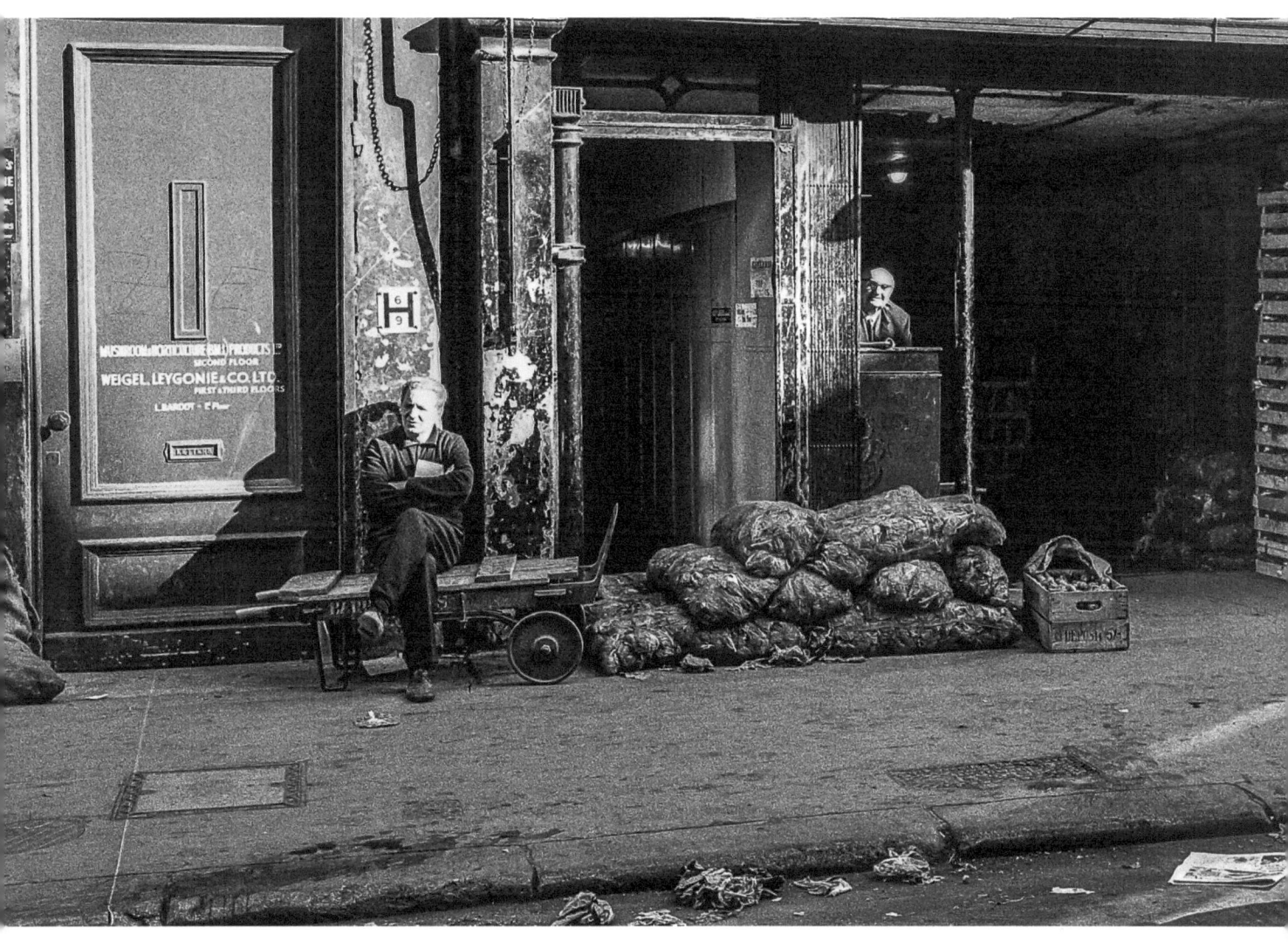

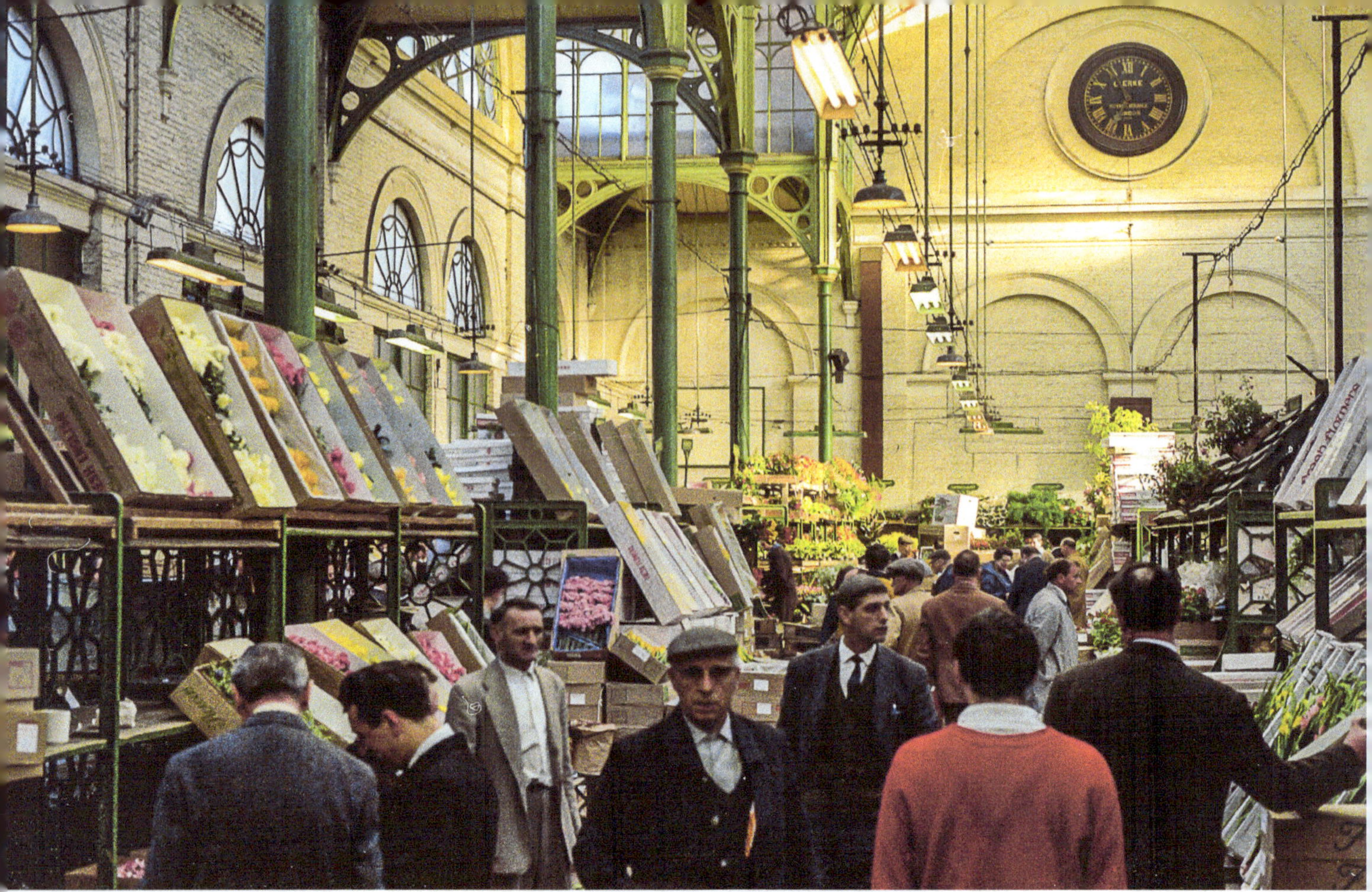

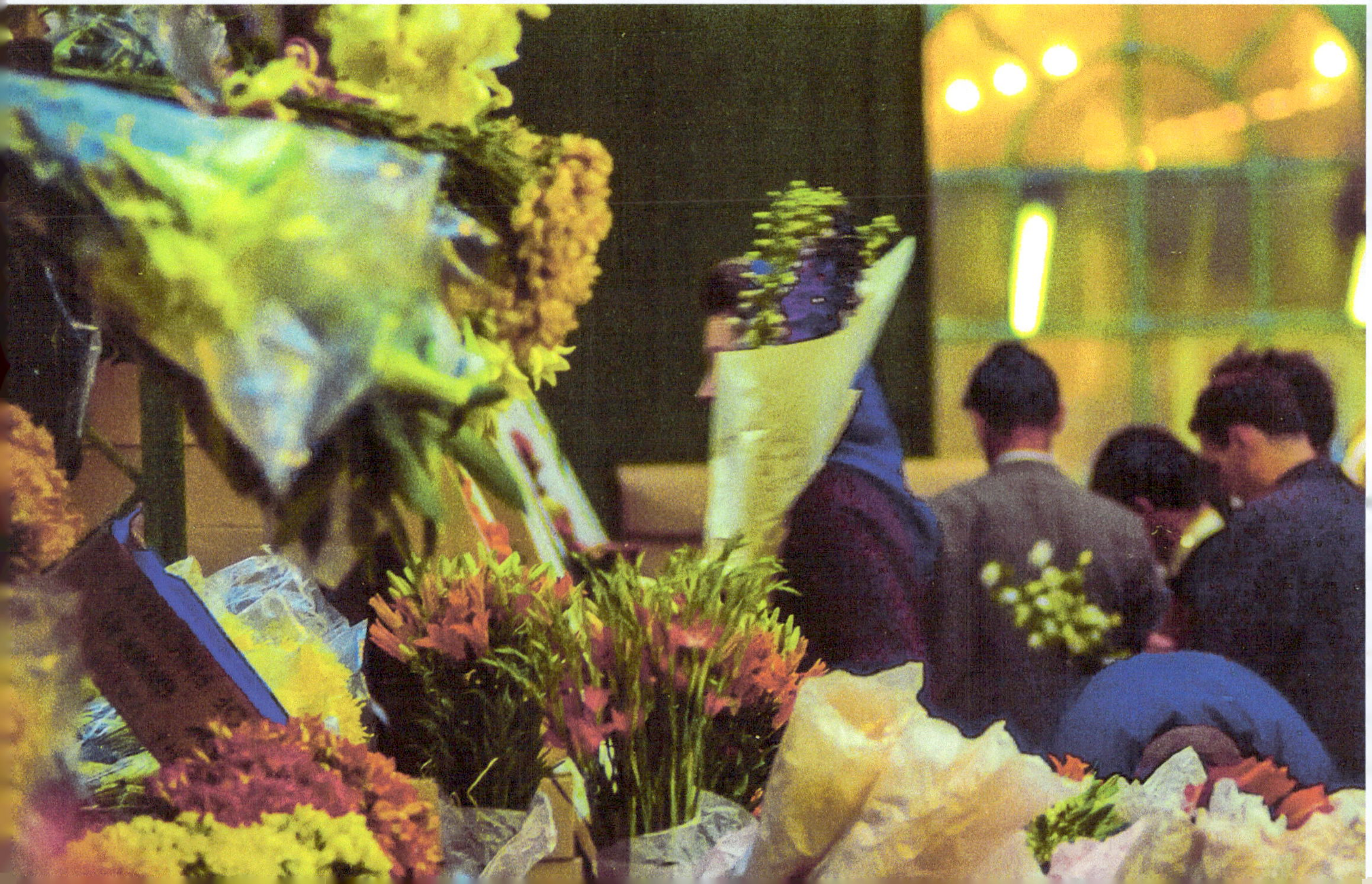

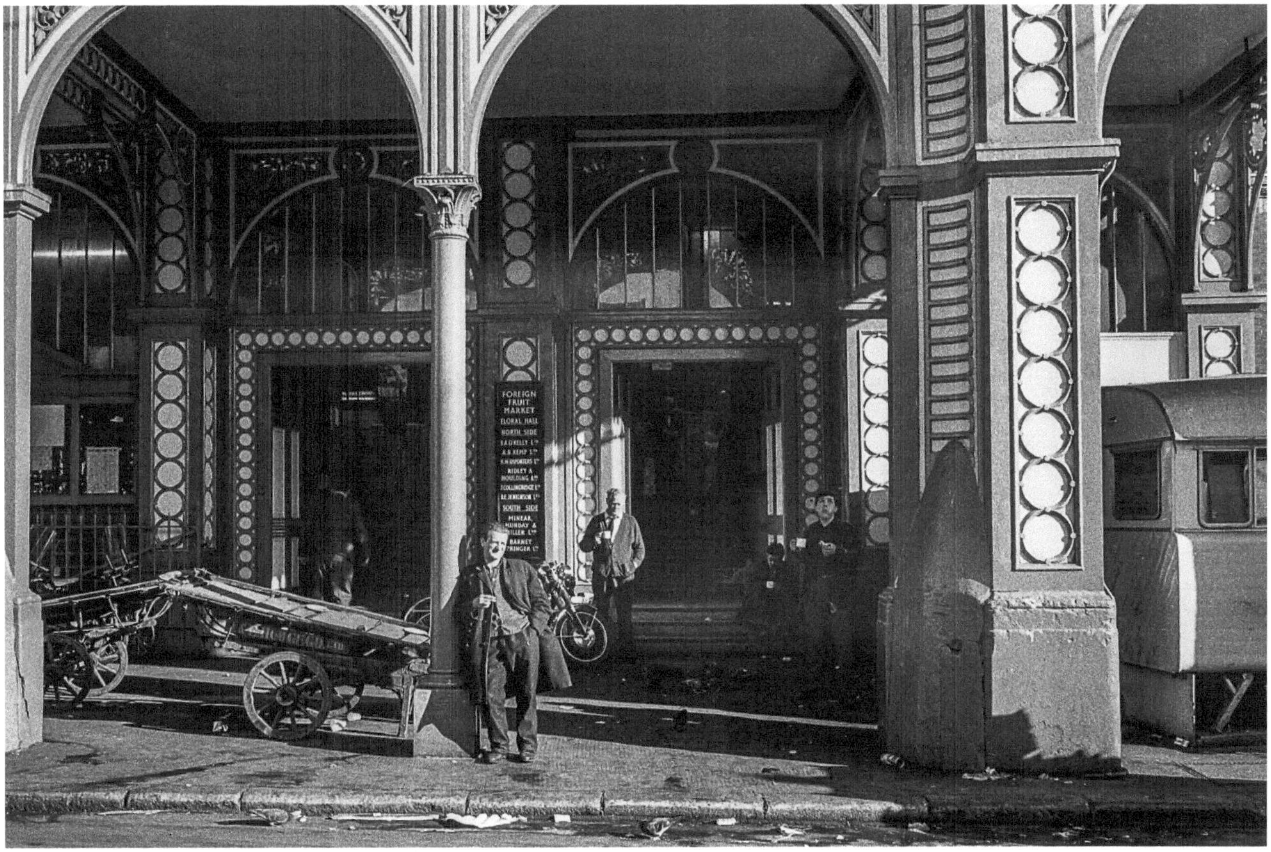

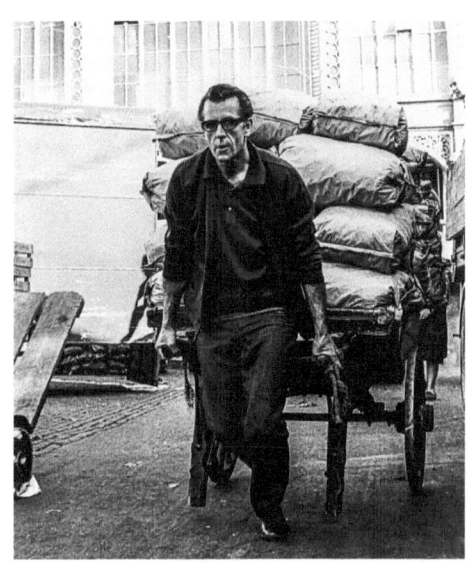

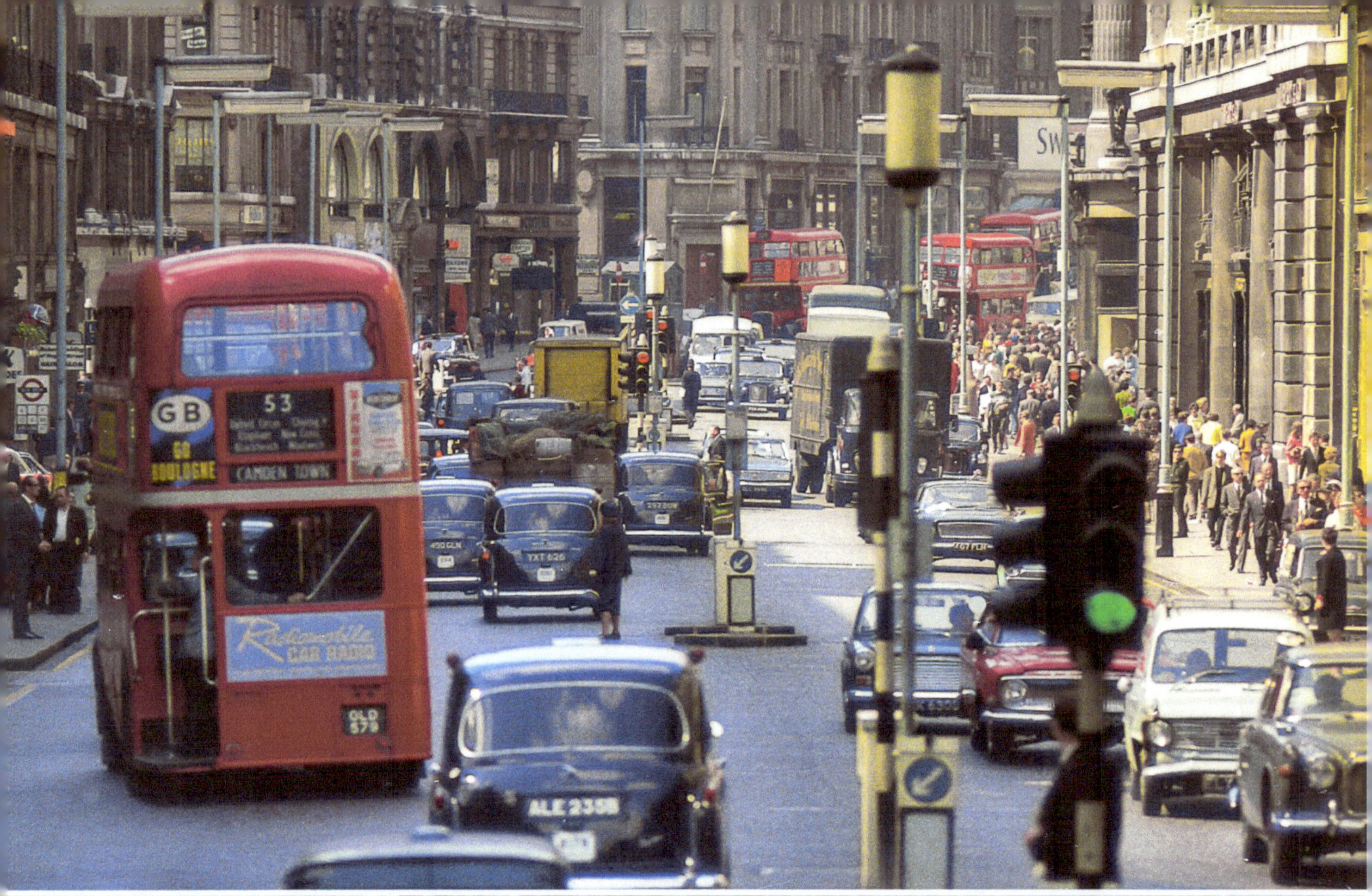

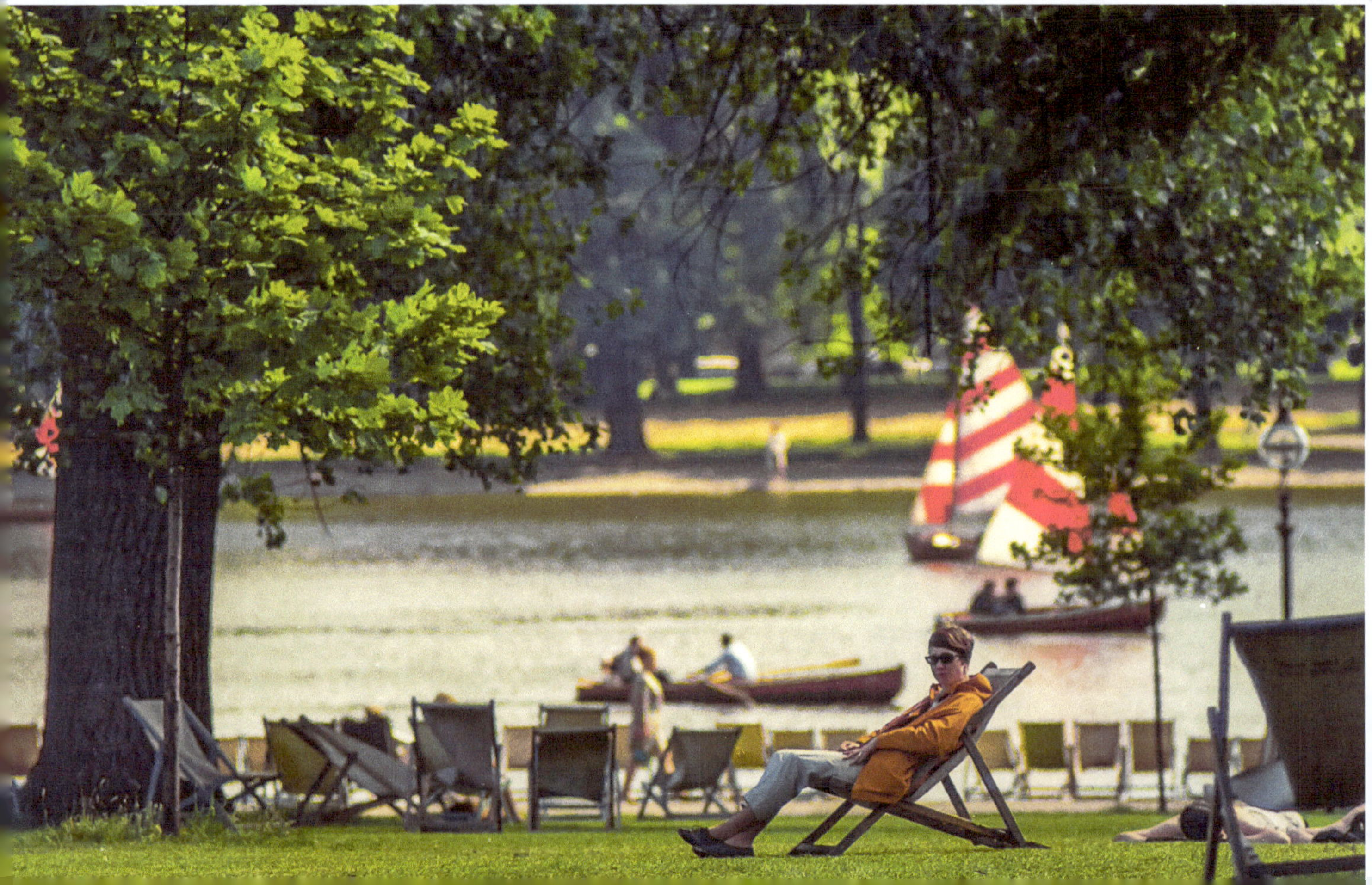

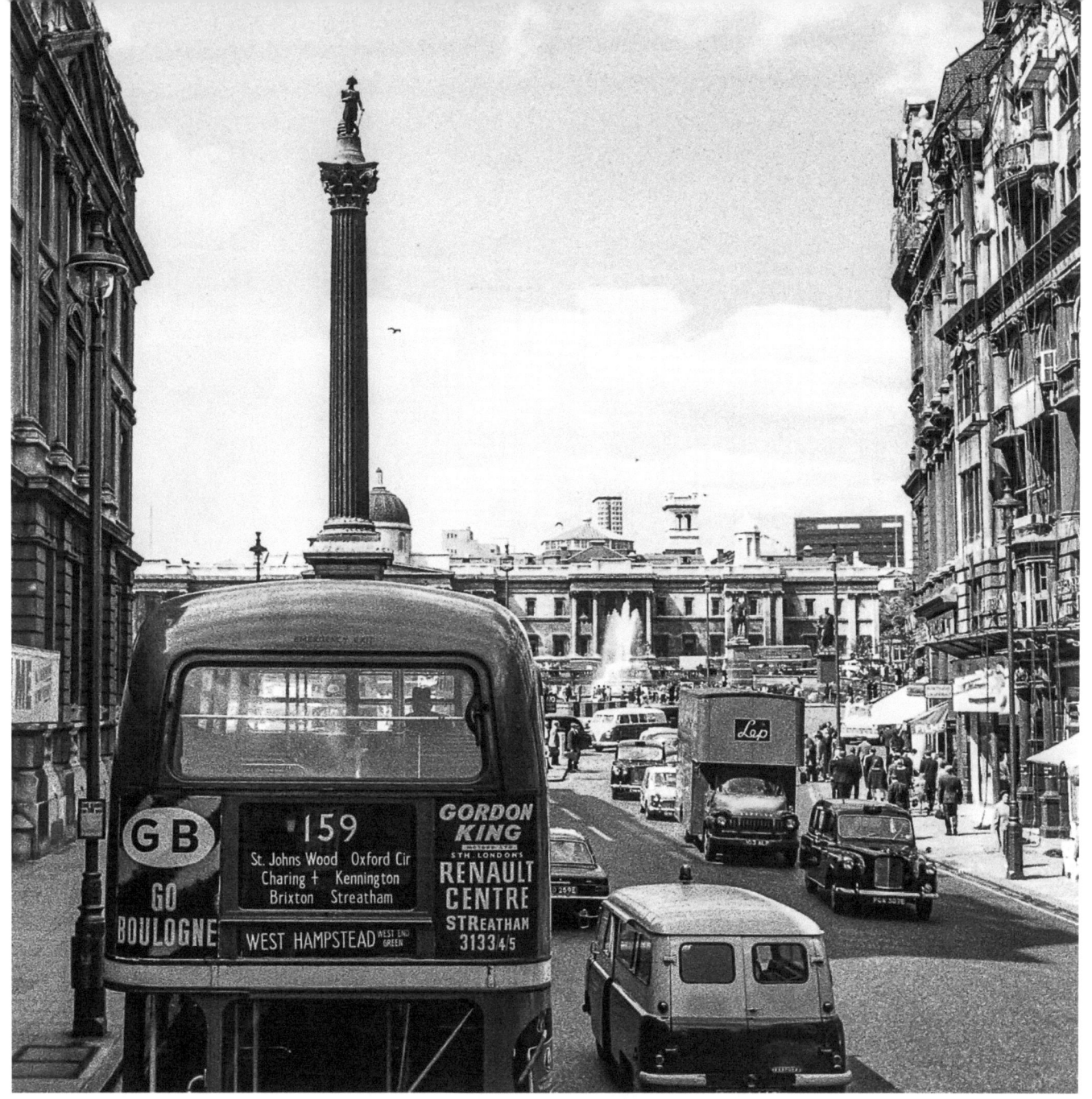

AROUND LONDON

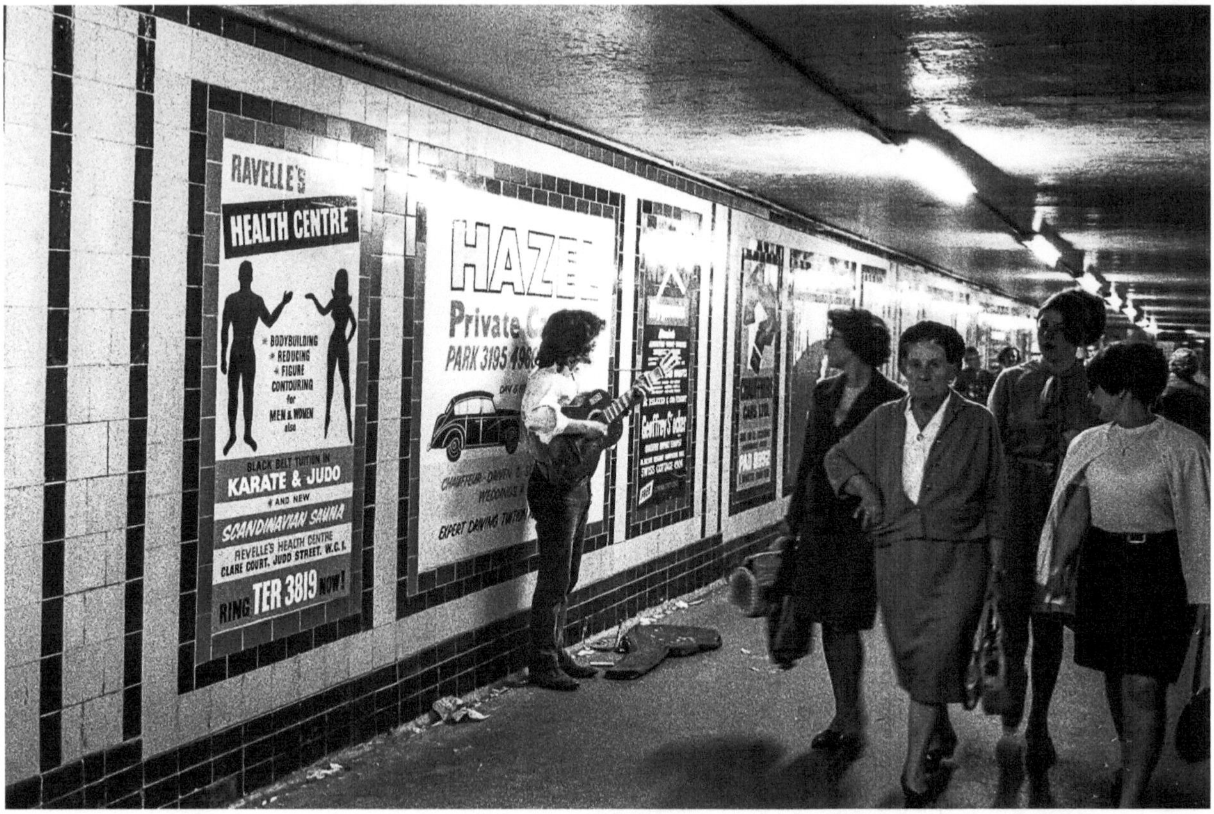

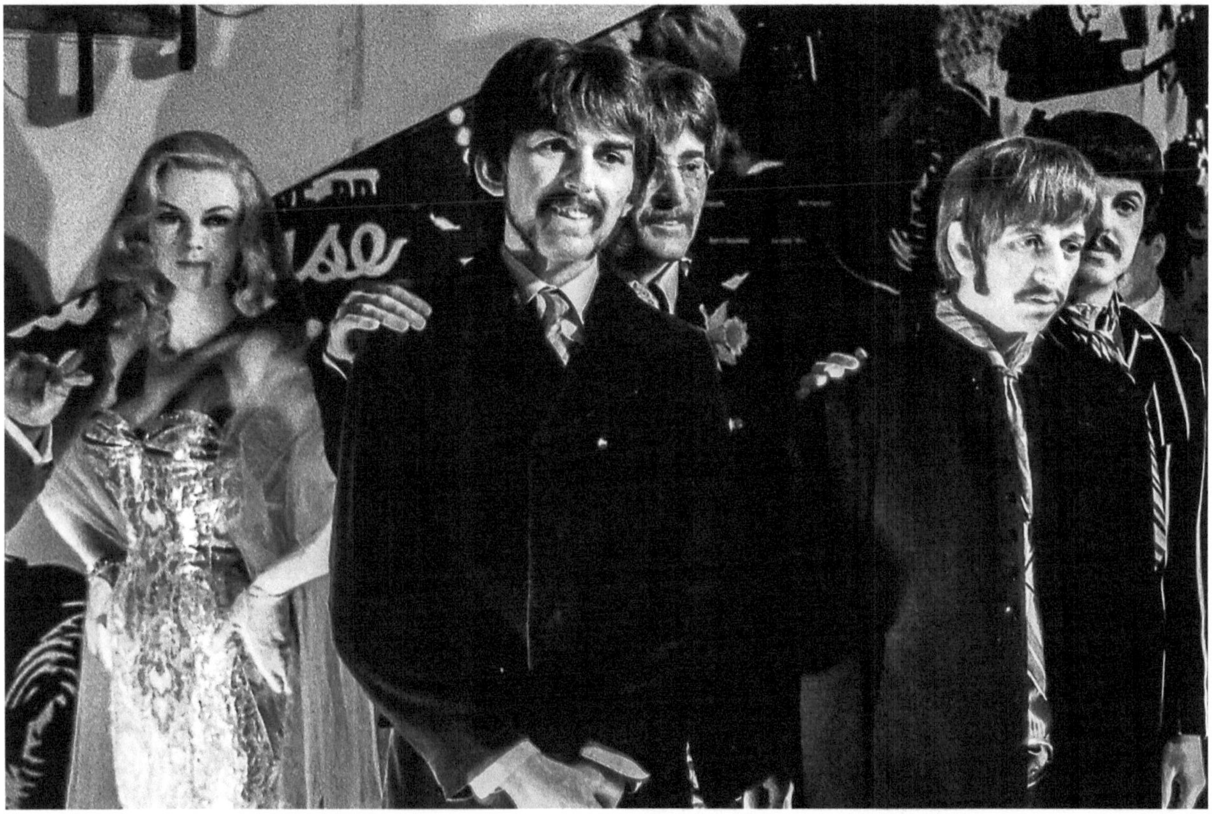

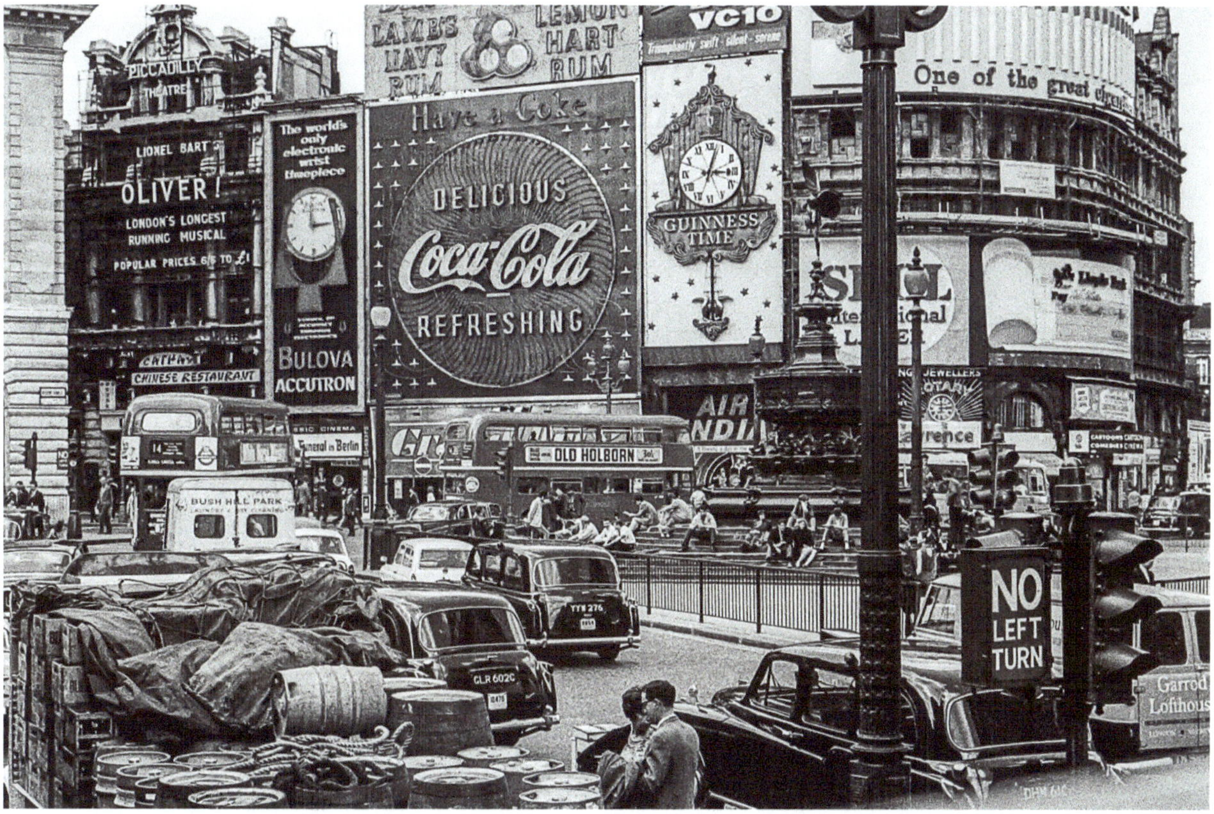

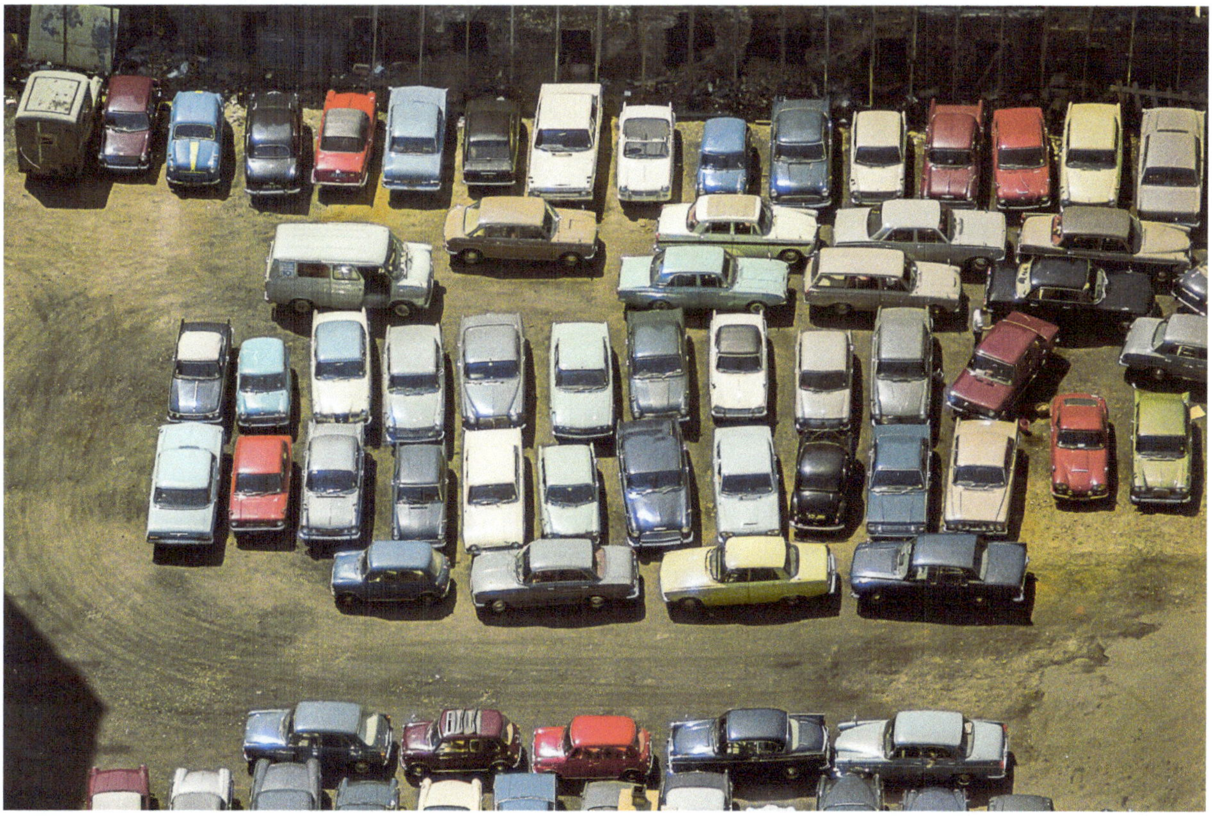

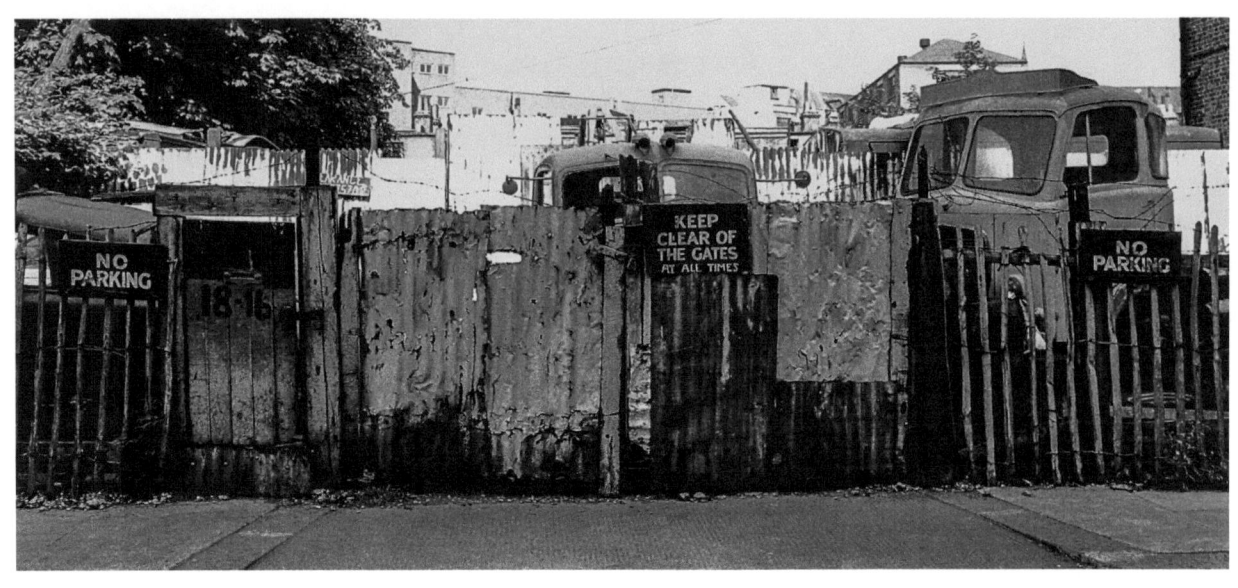

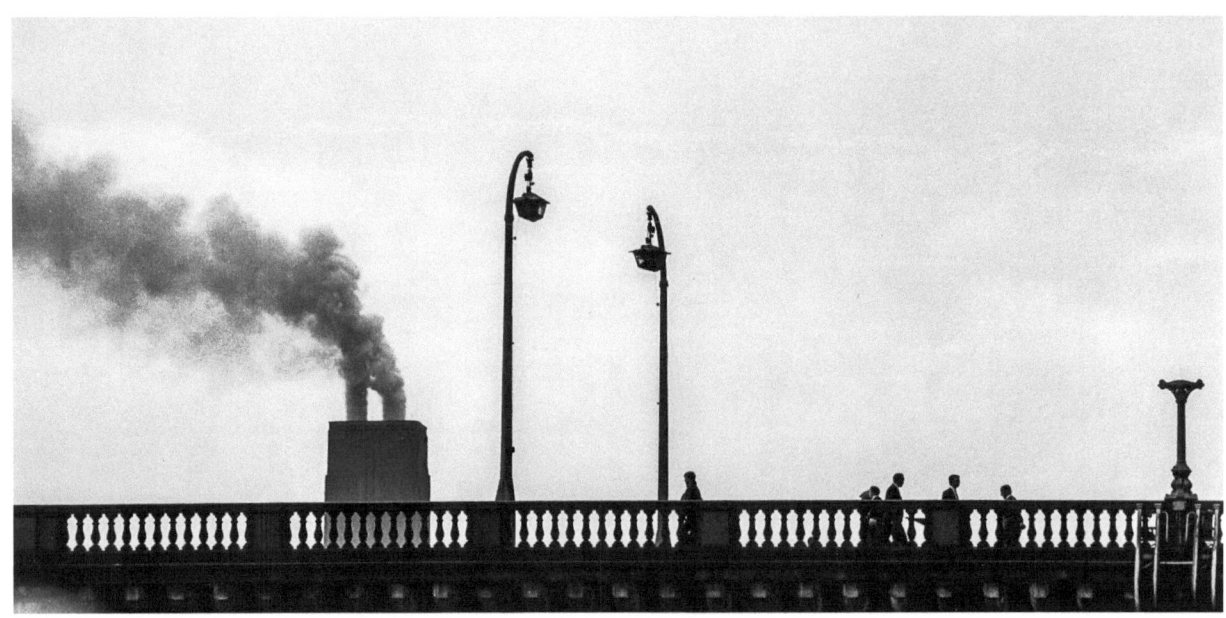

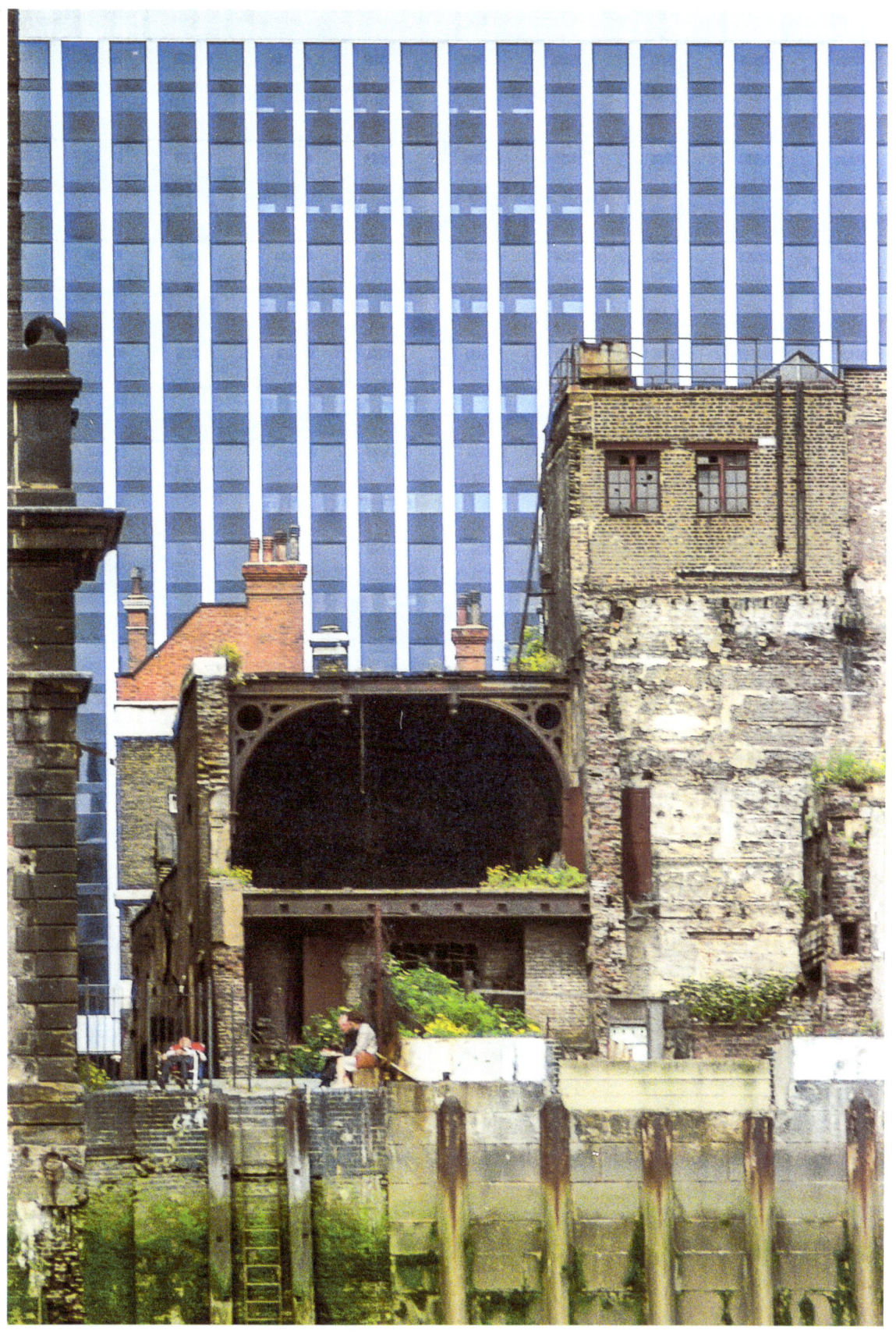

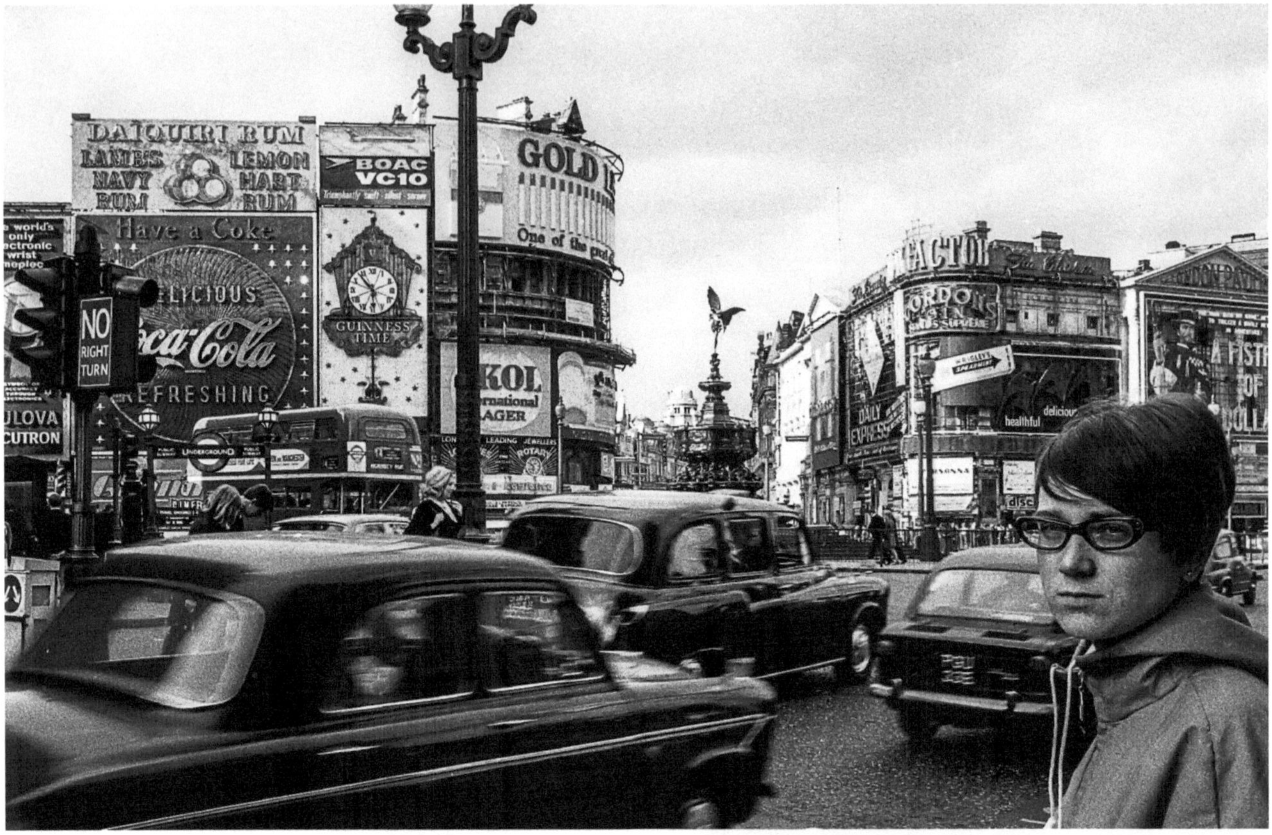

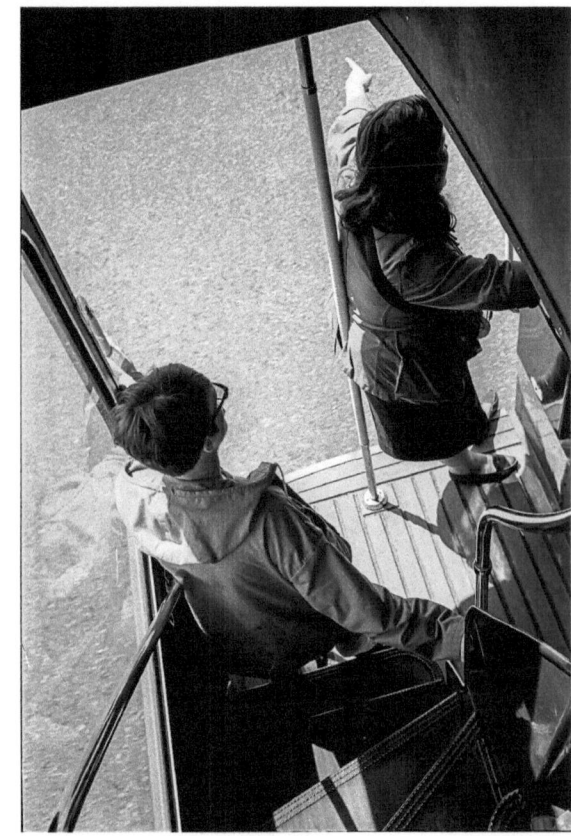

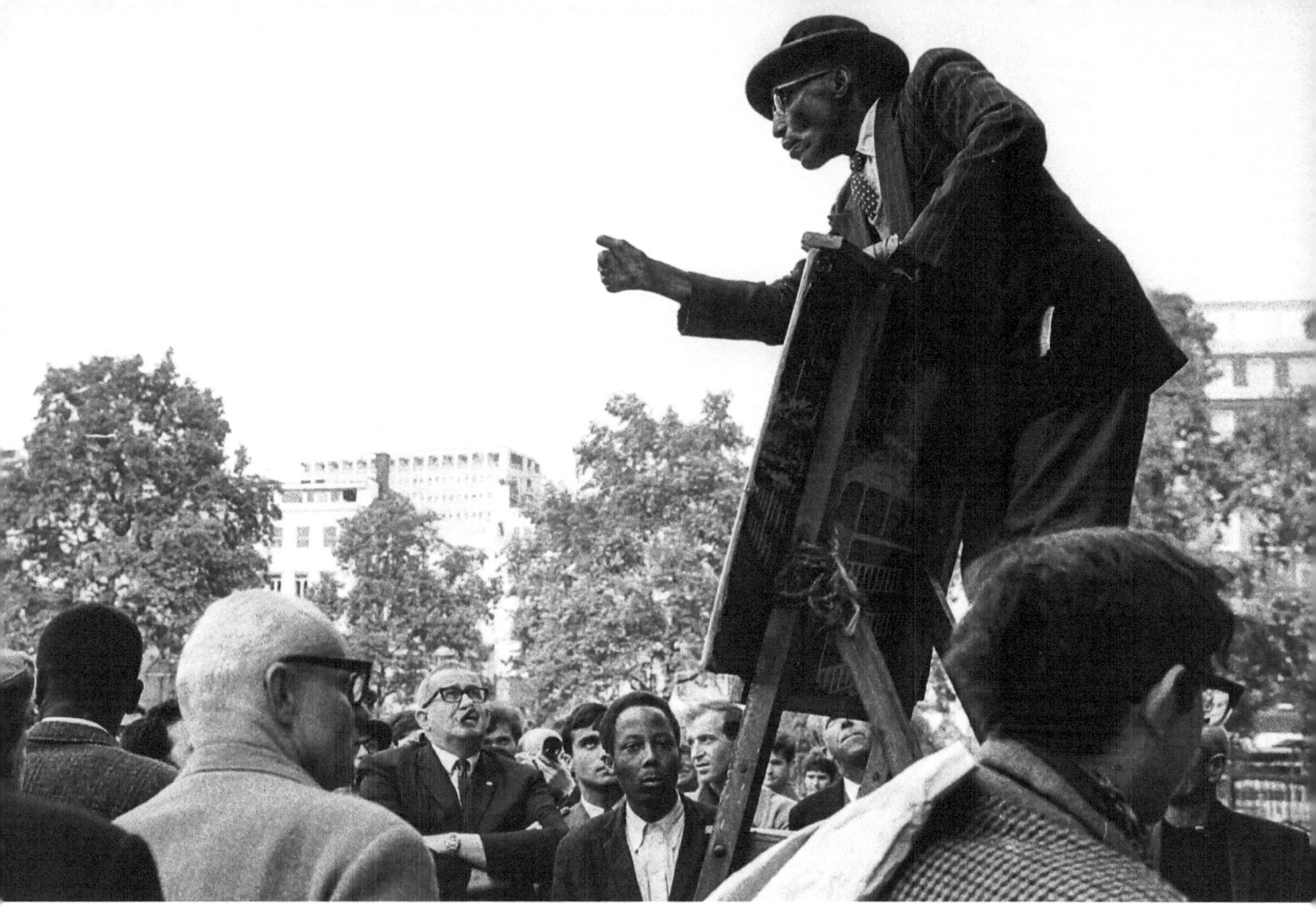

SPEAKERS CORNER

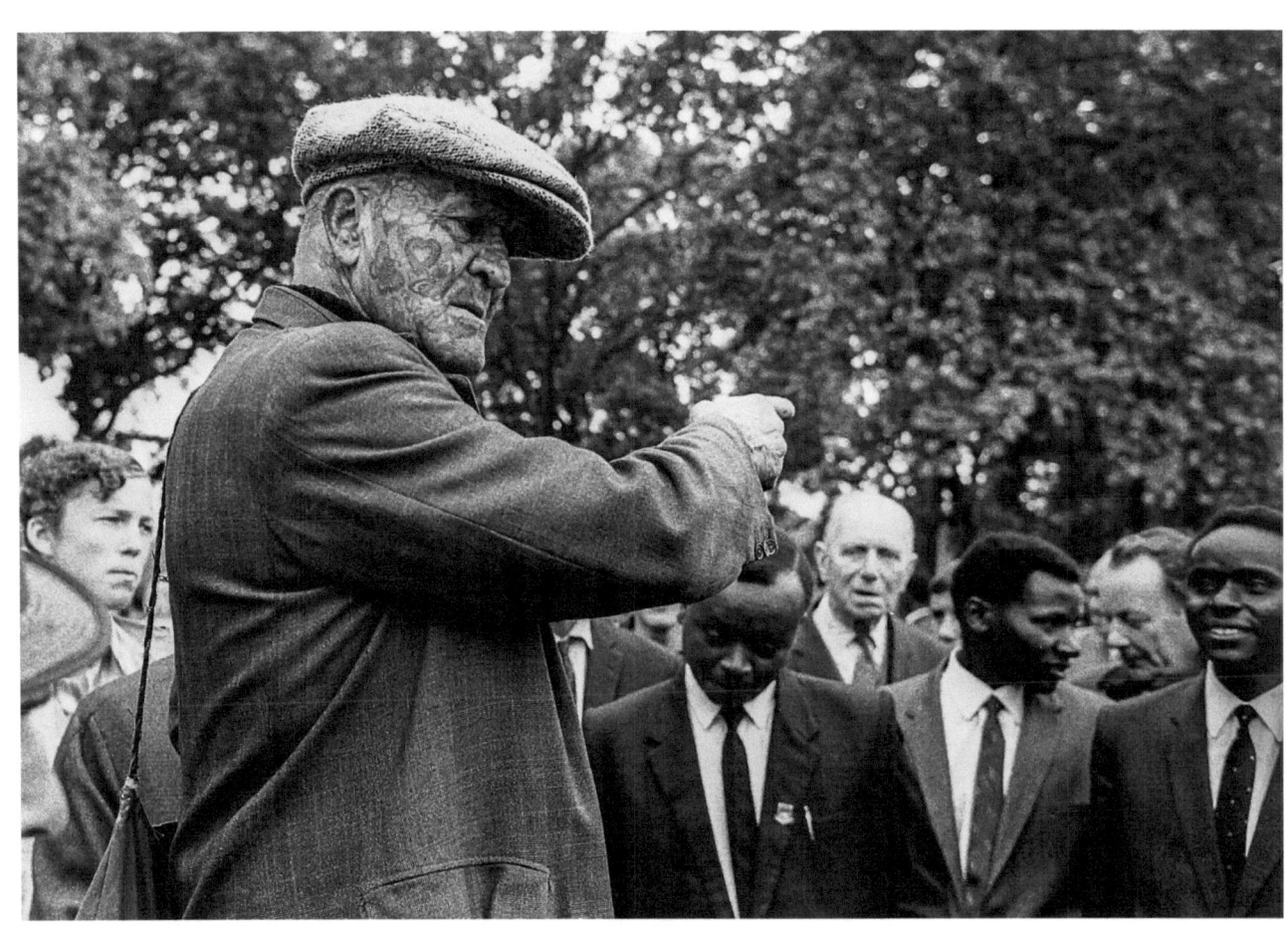

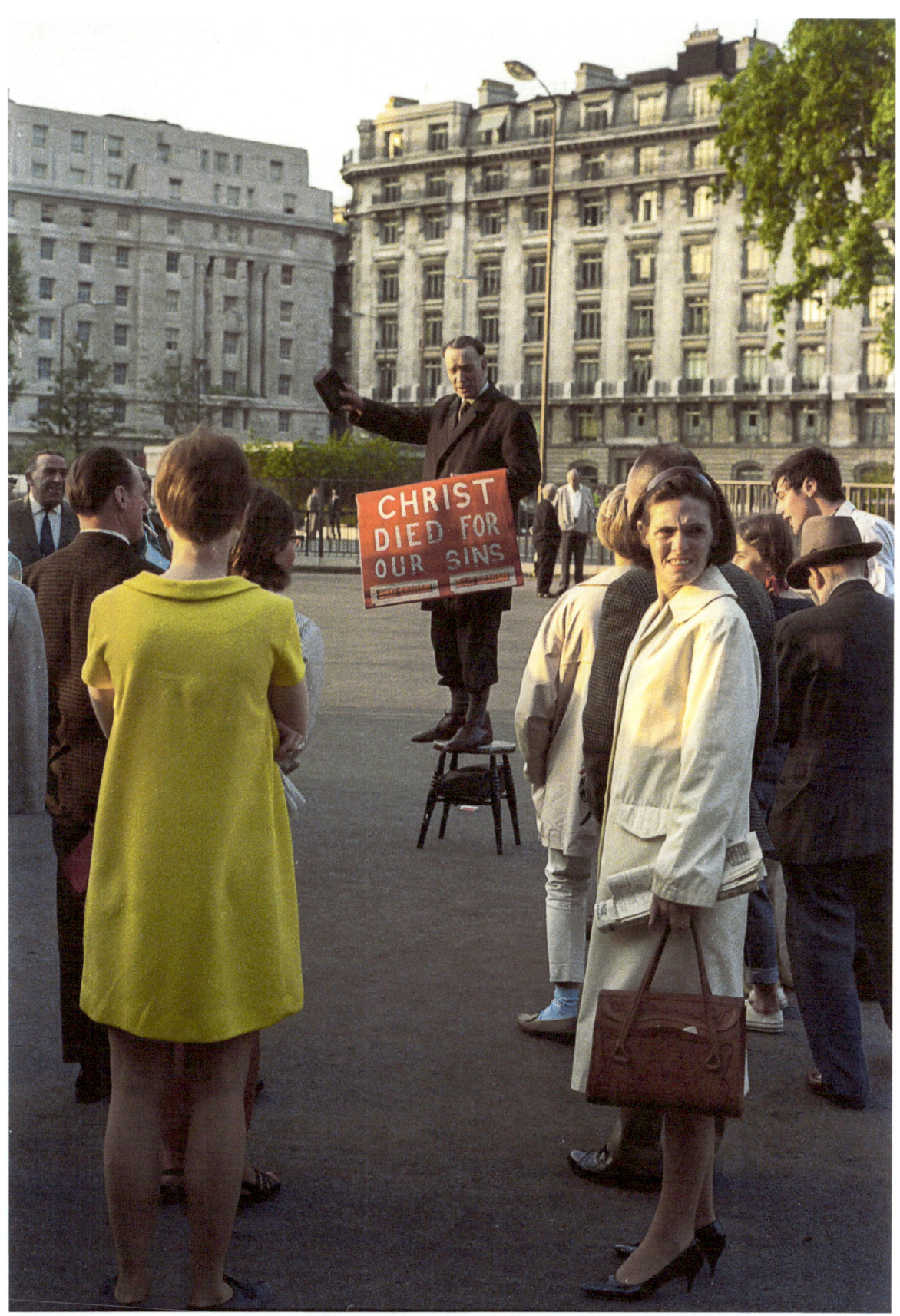

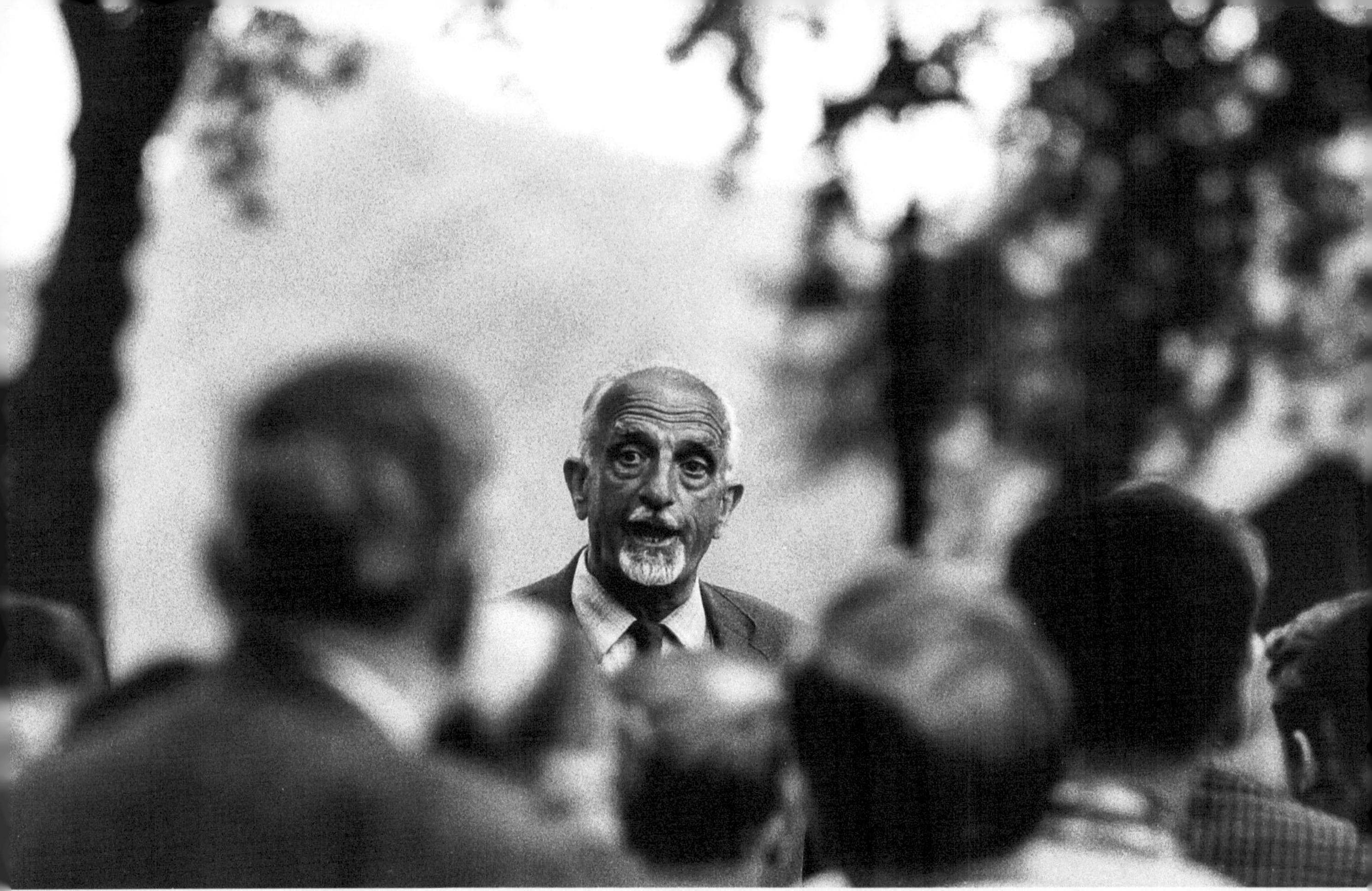

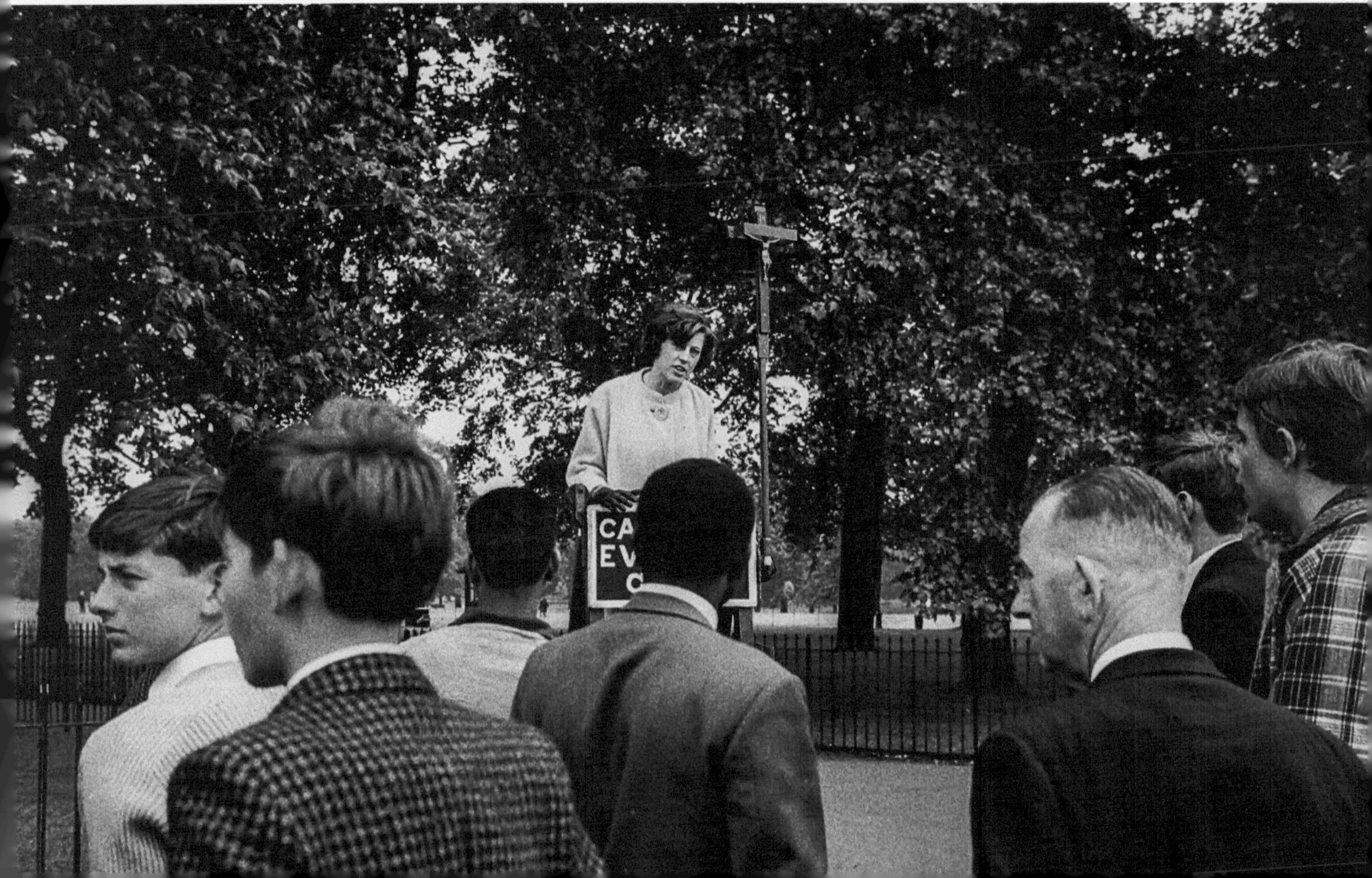

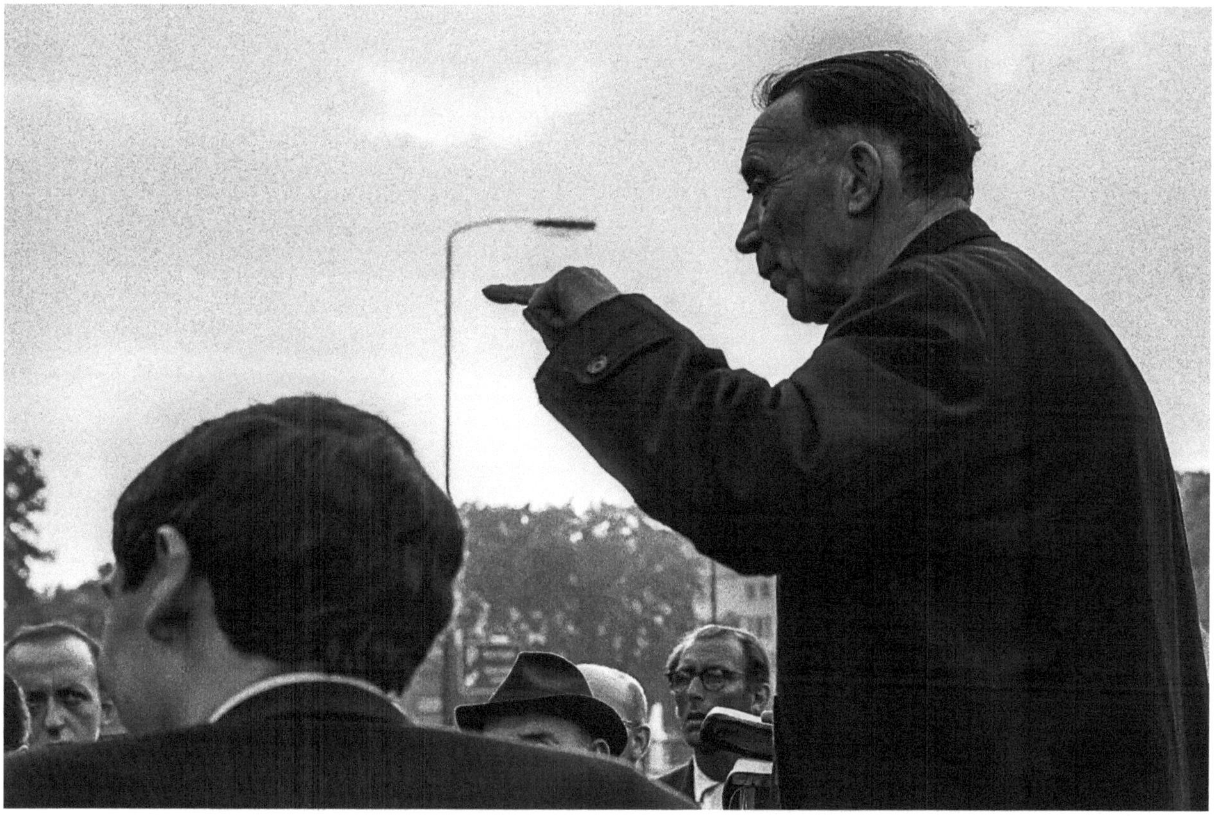

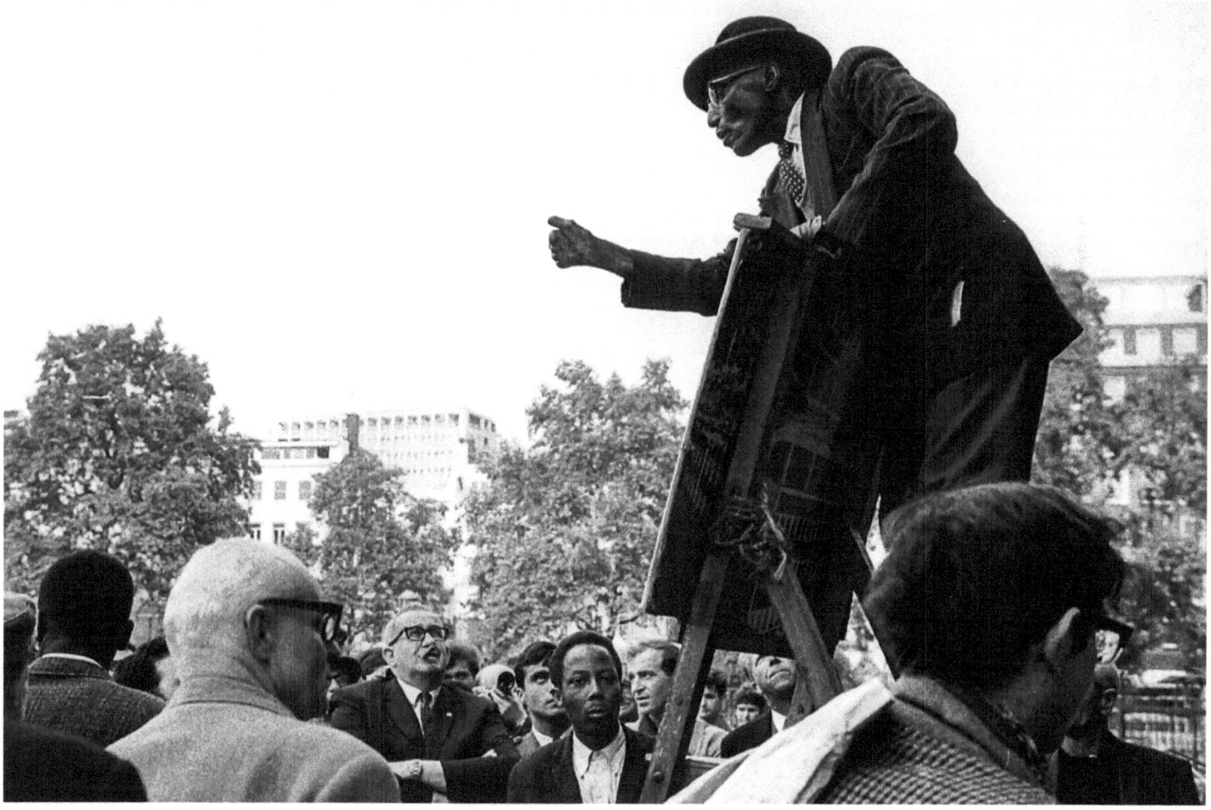

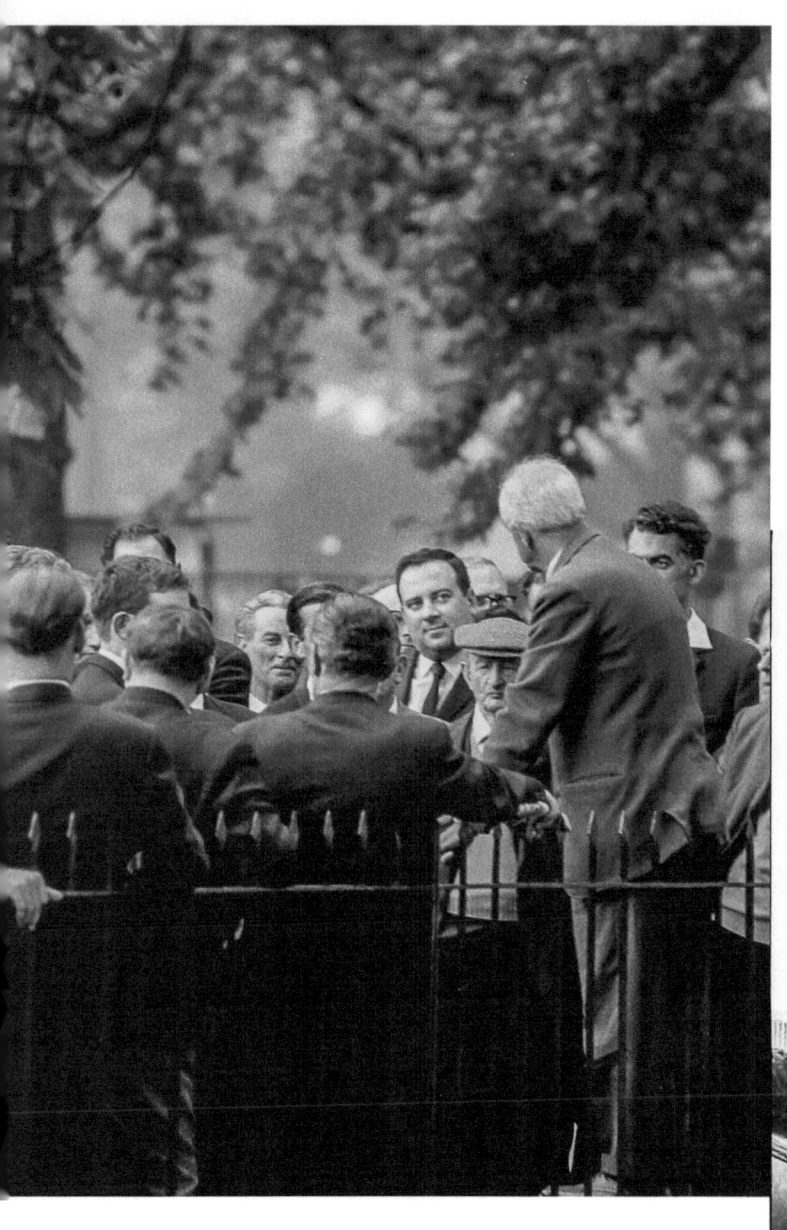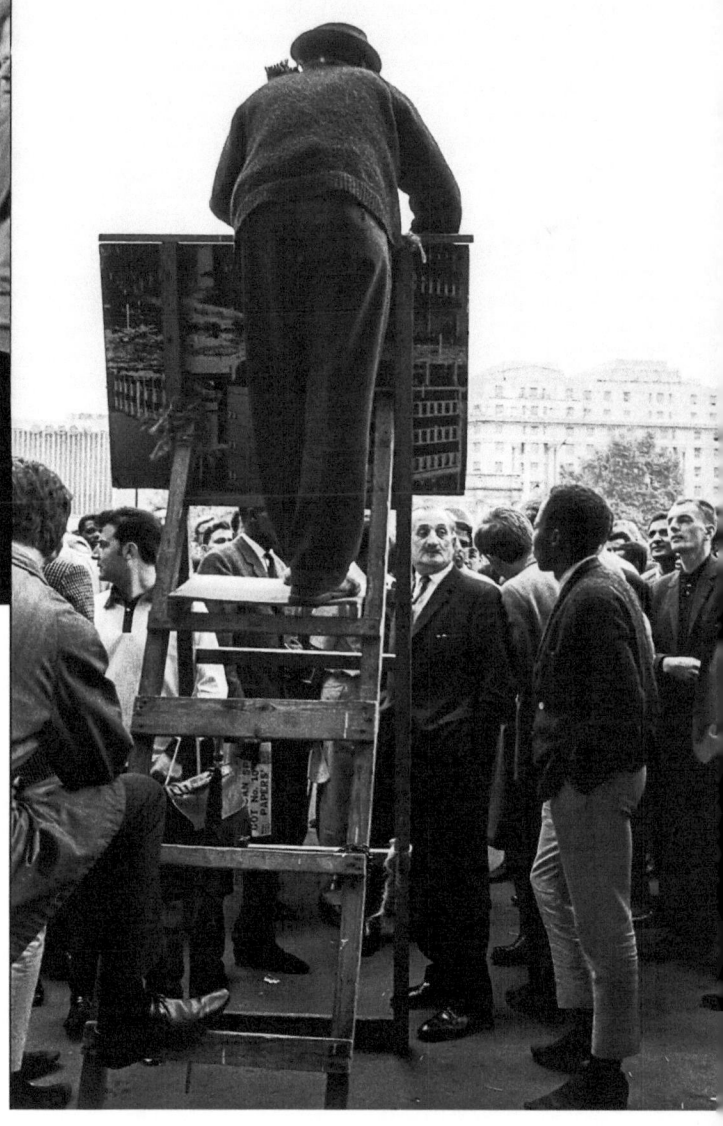

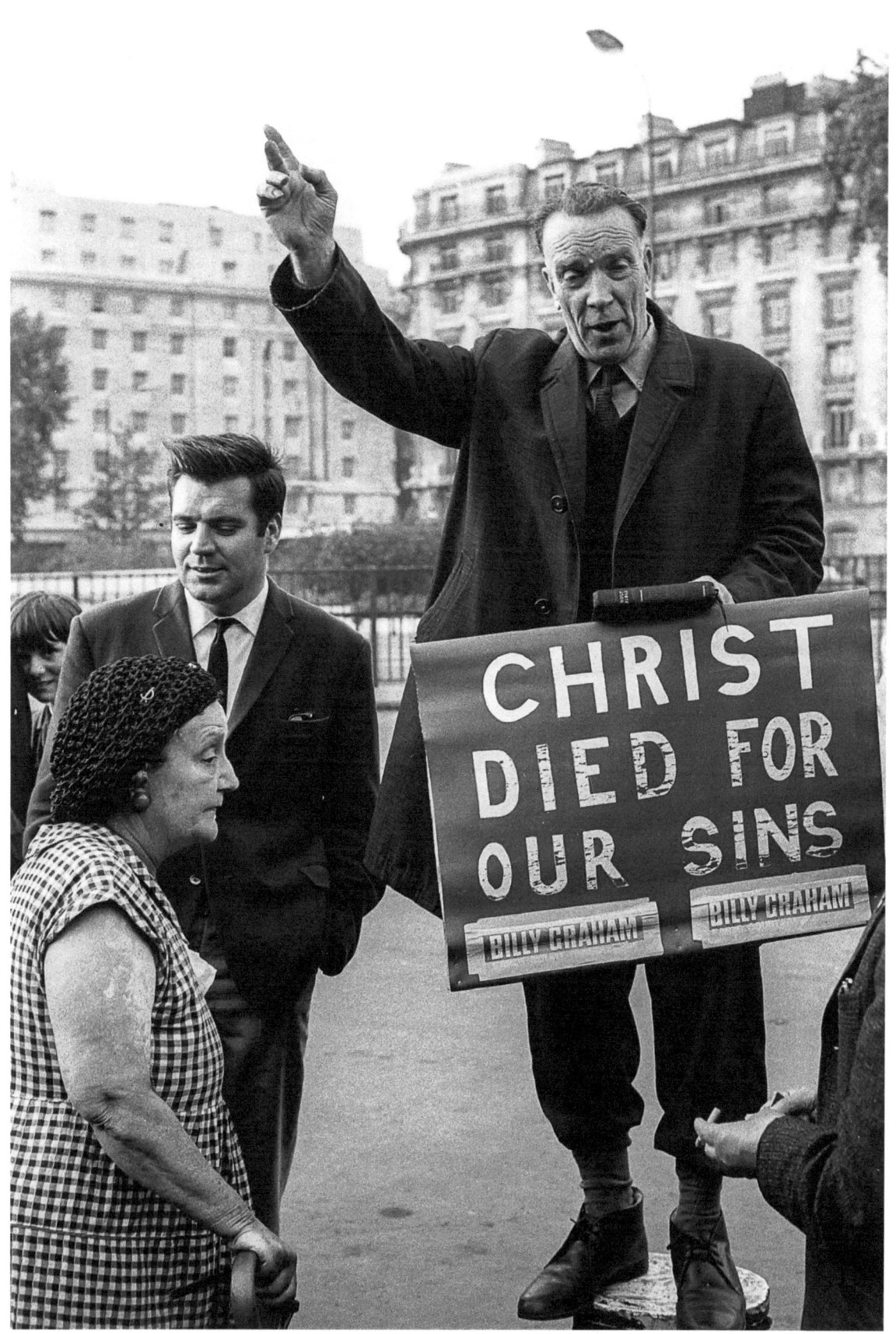

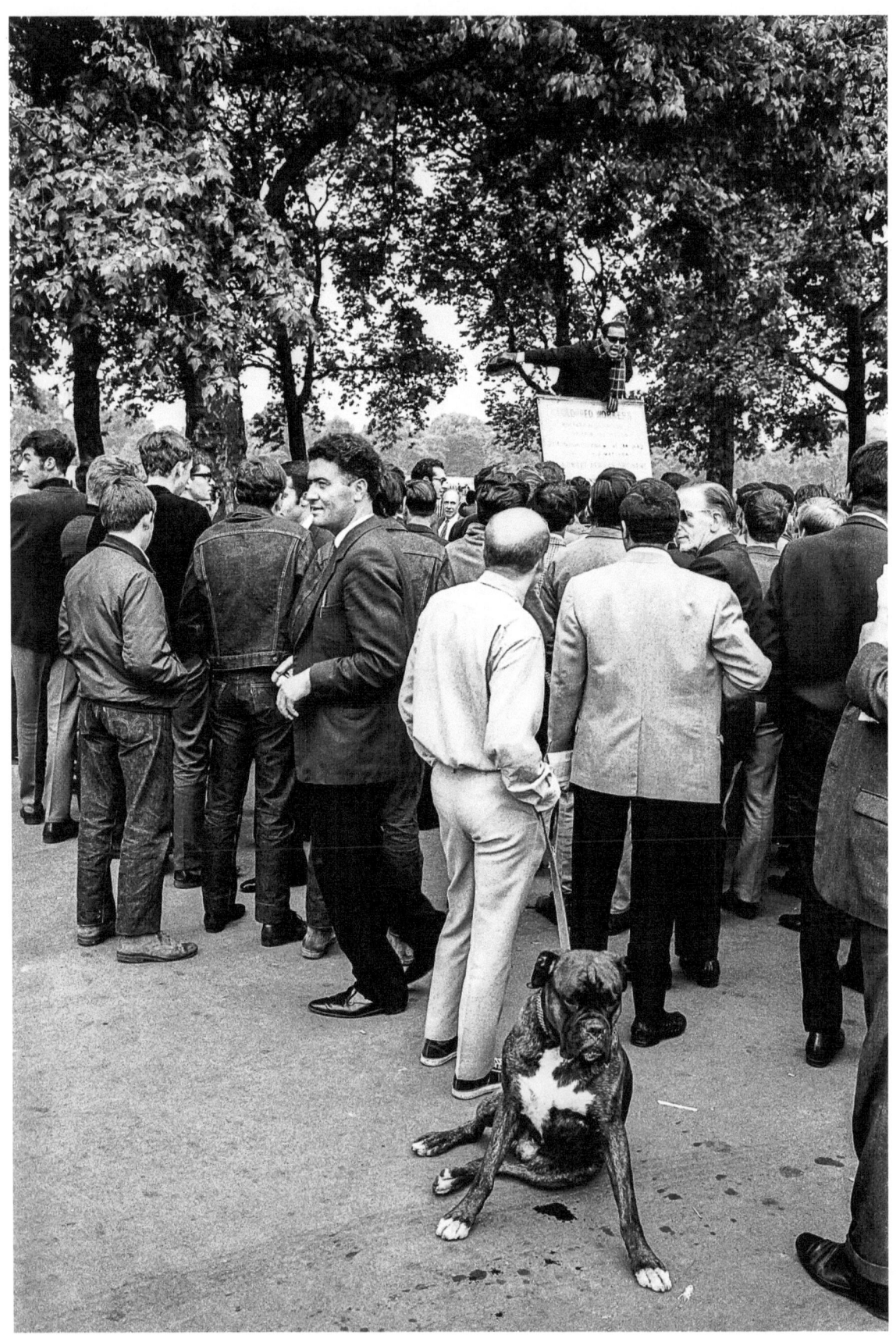

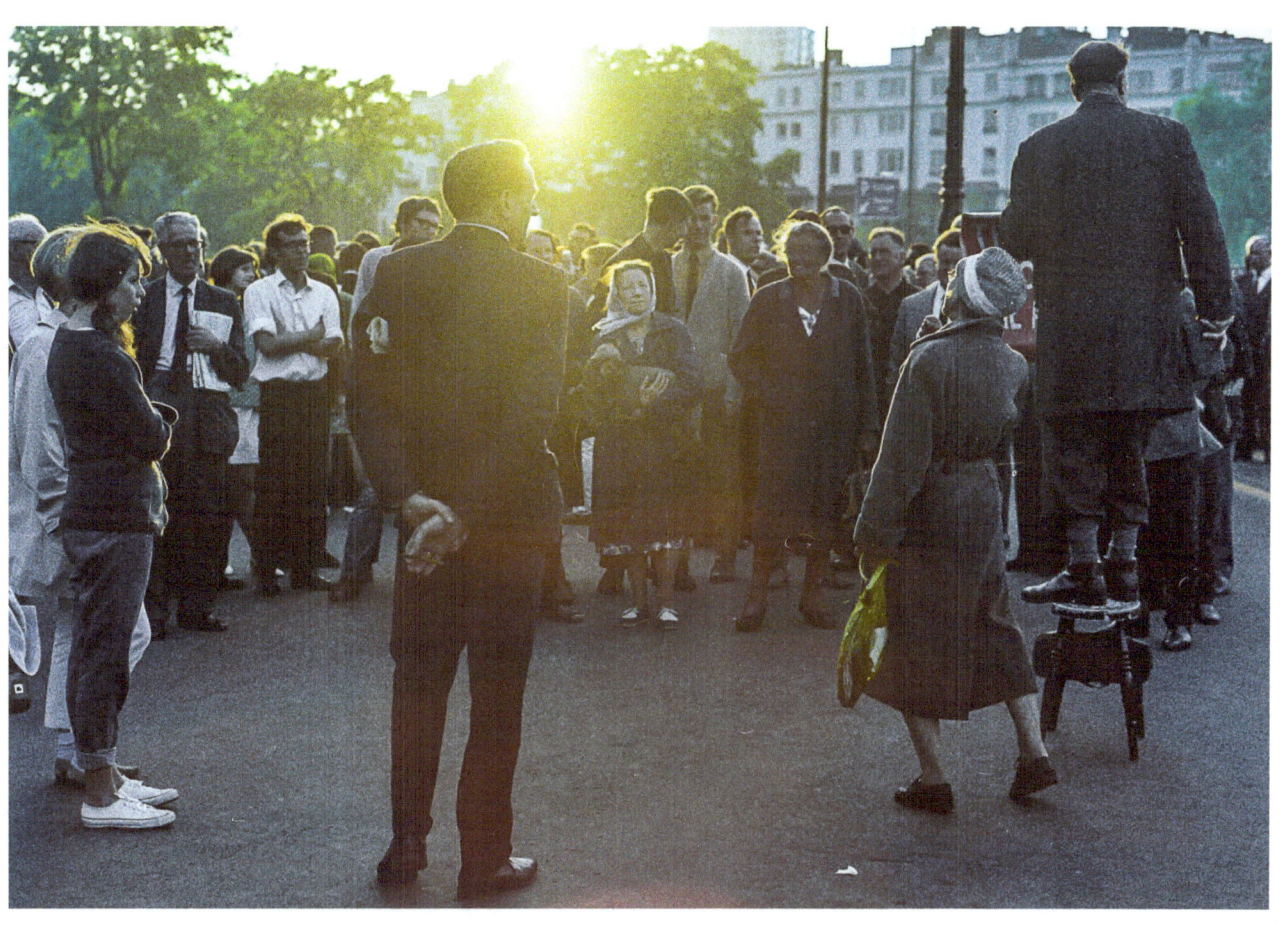

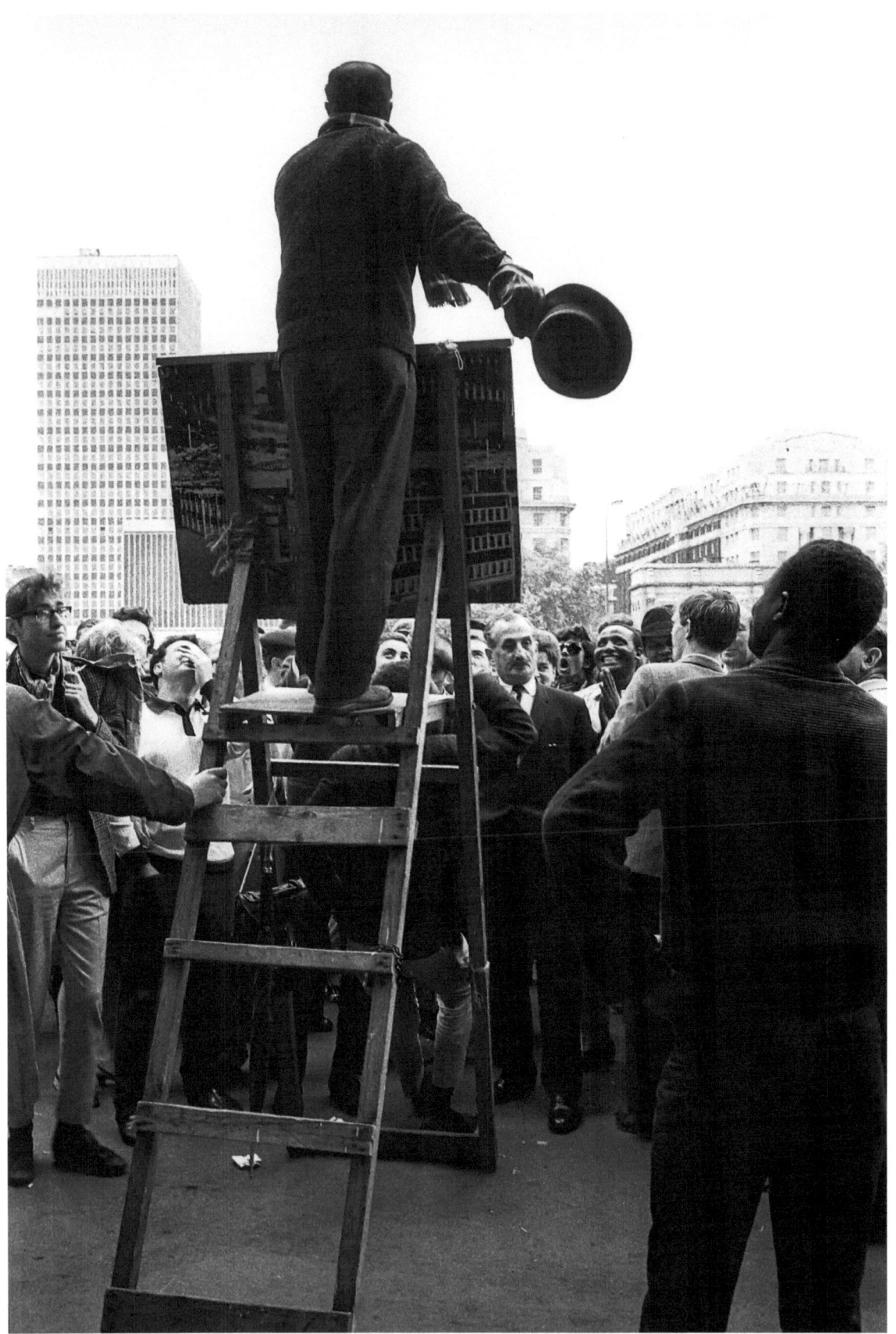

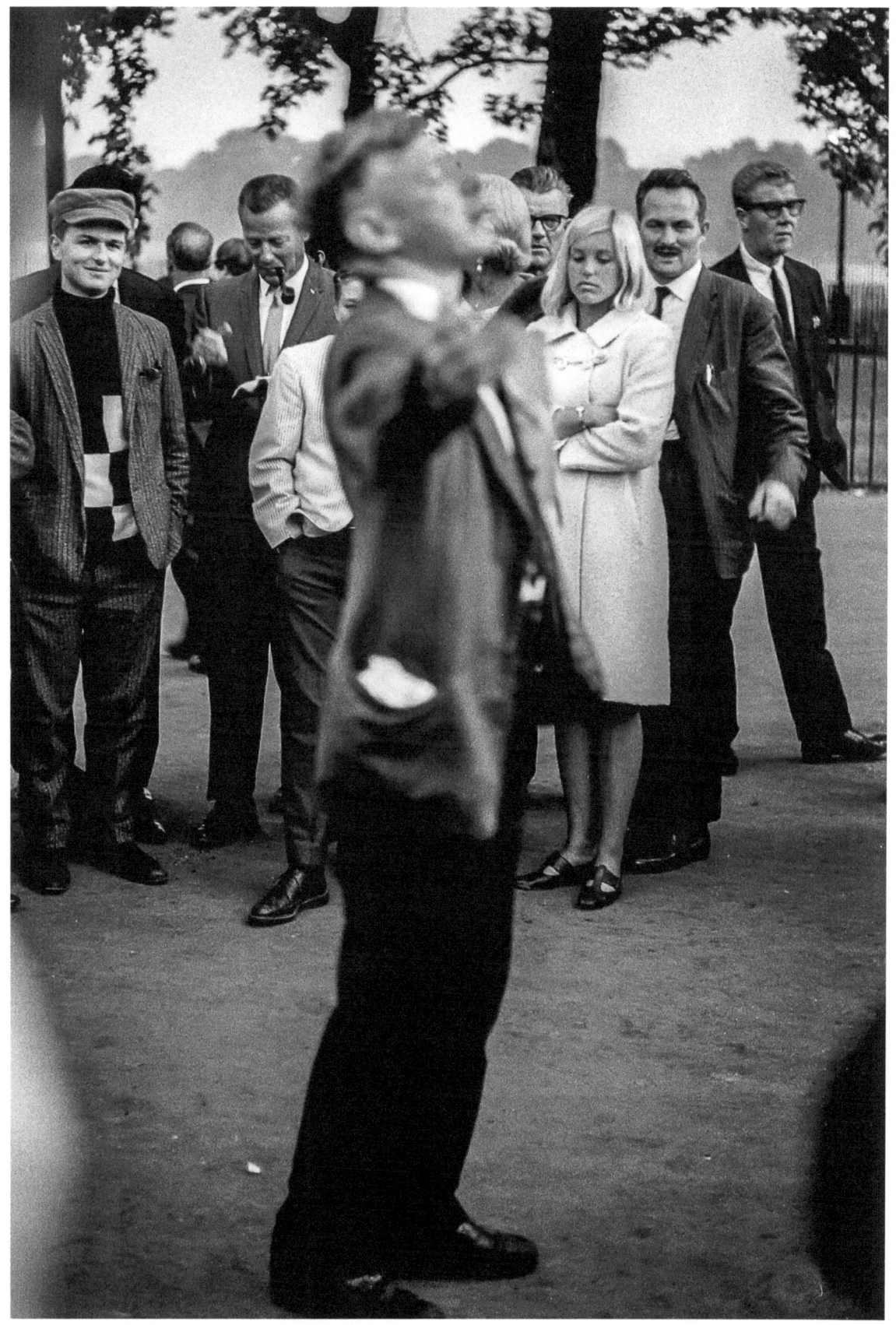

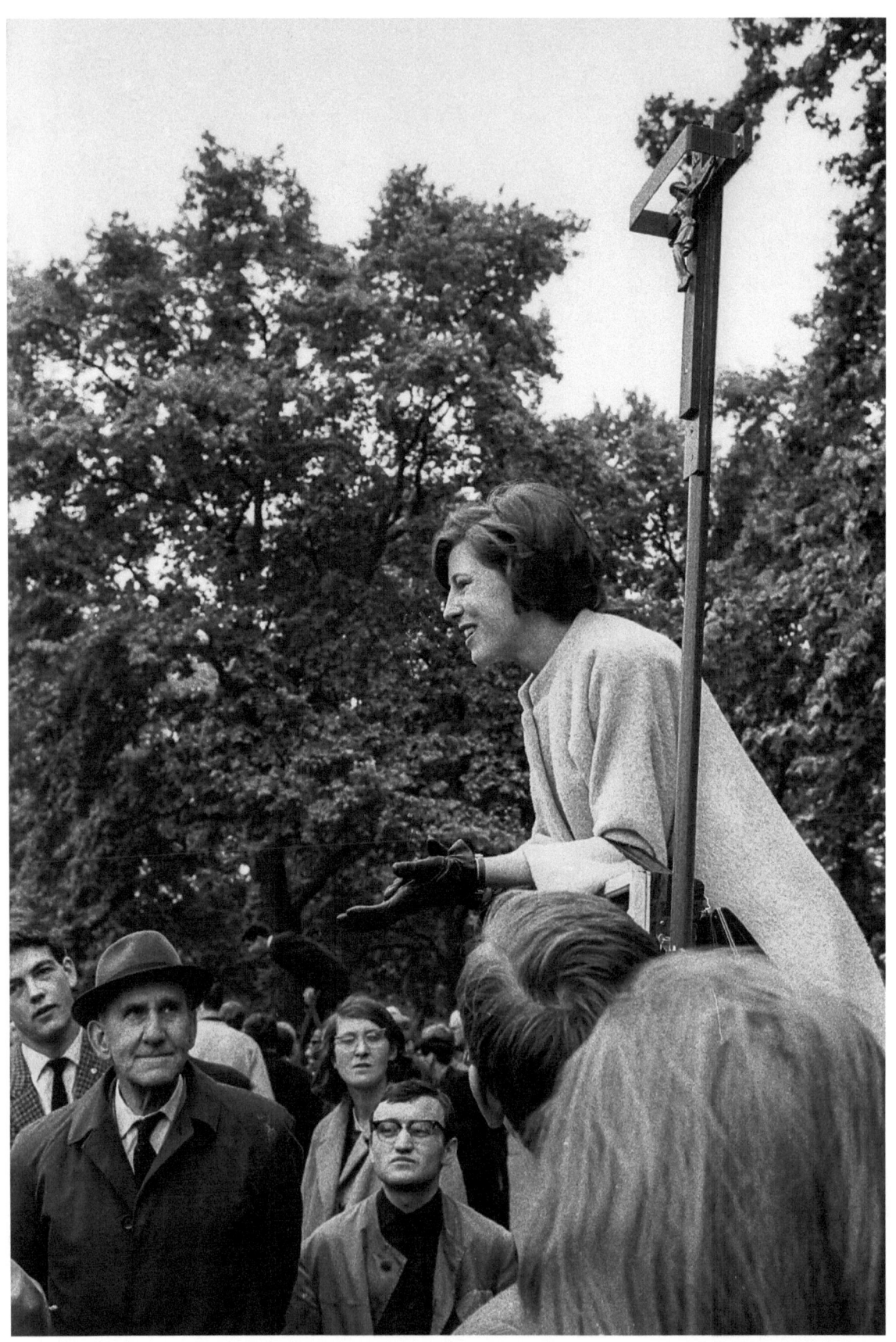

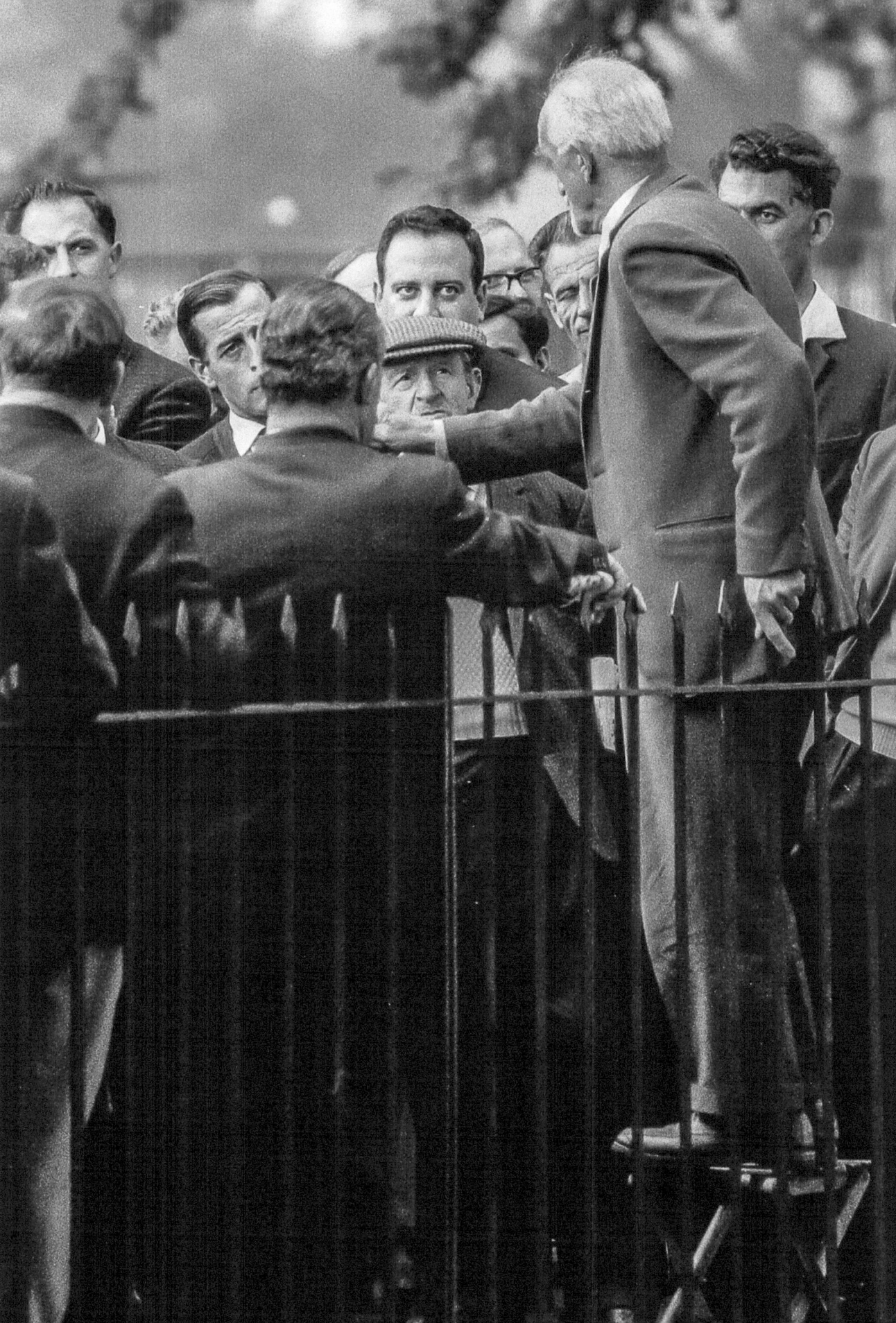

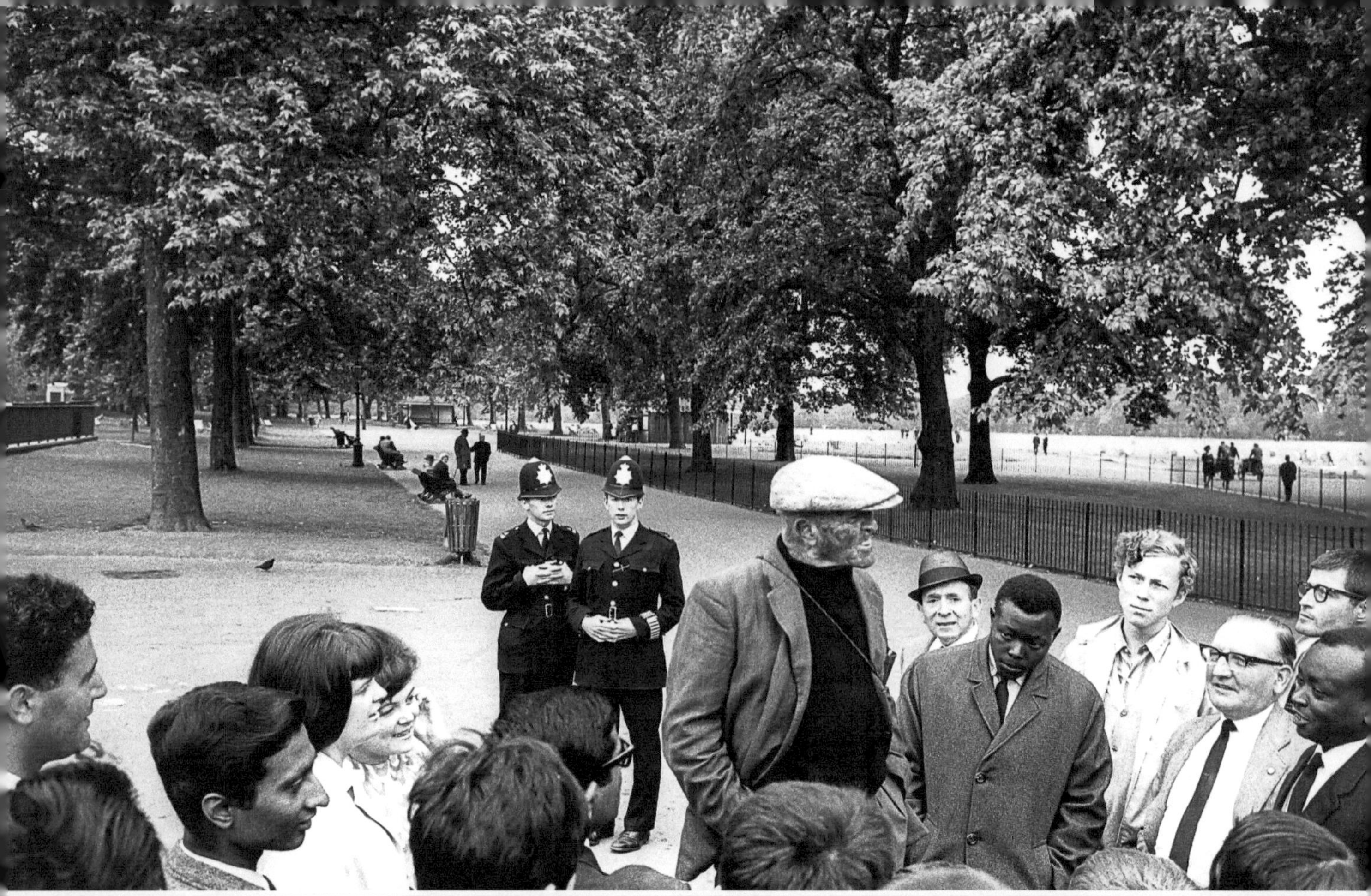

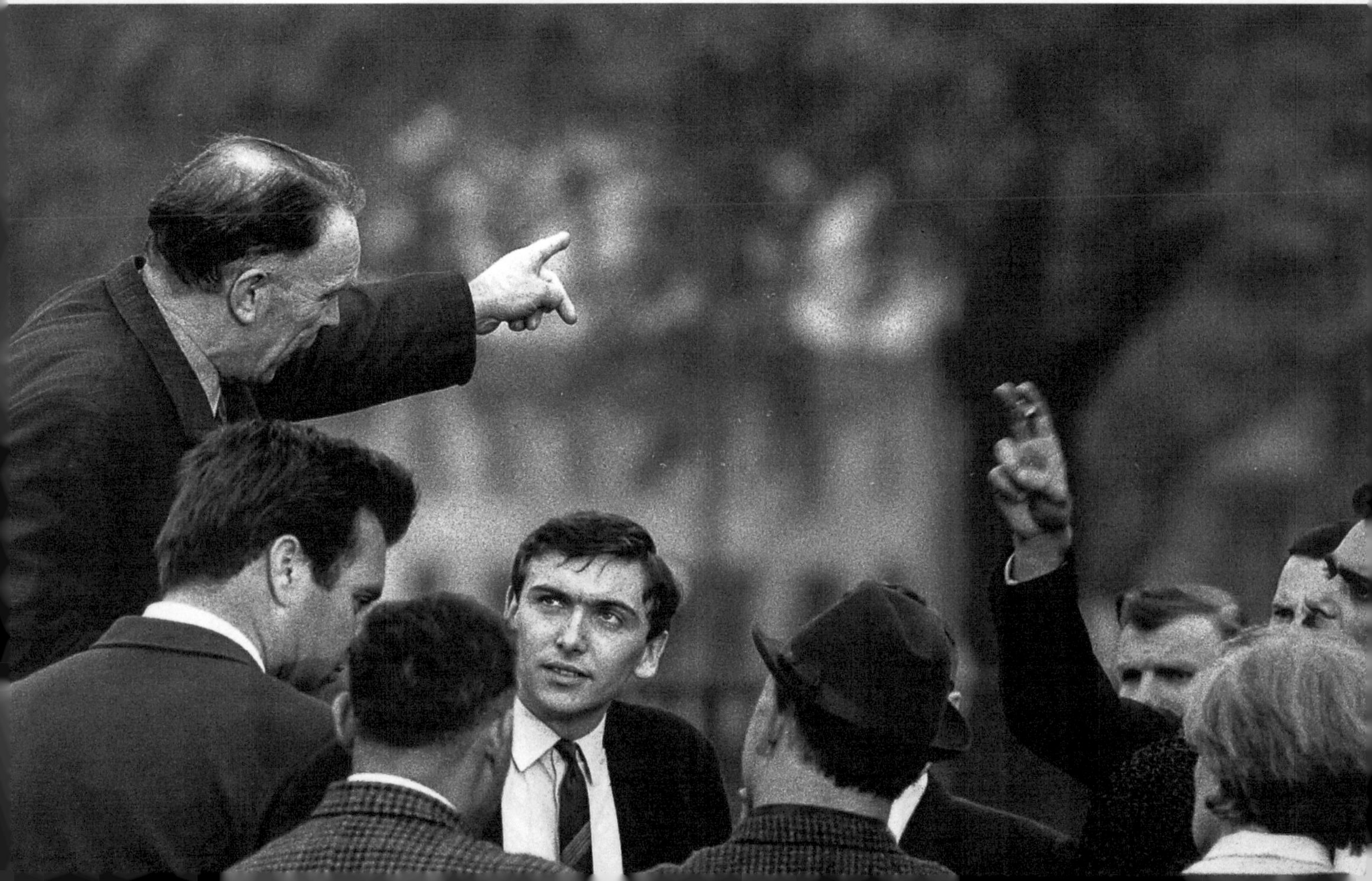

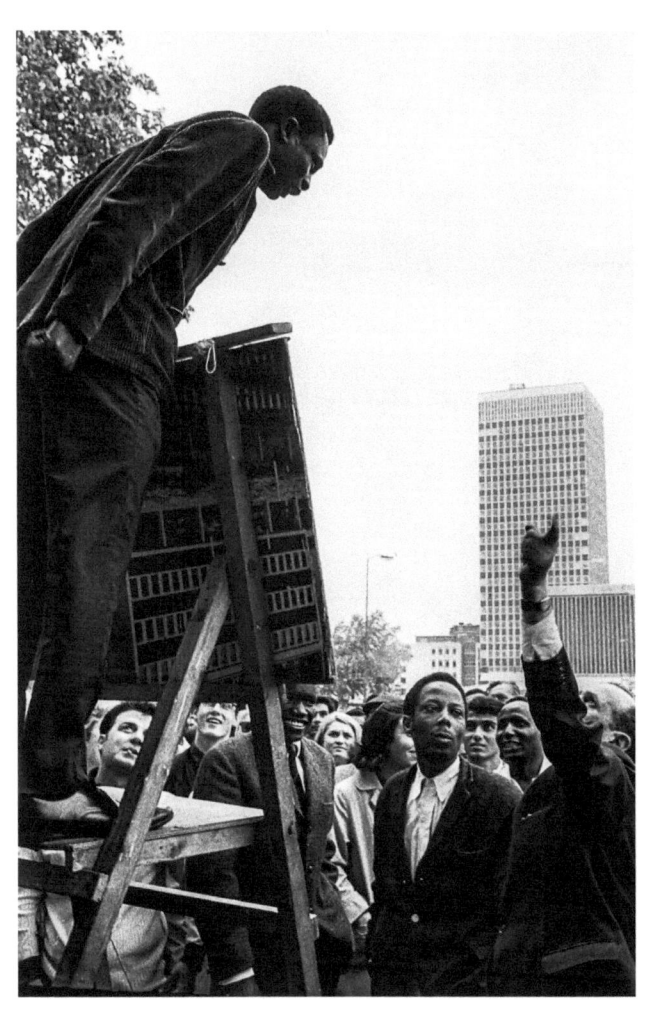

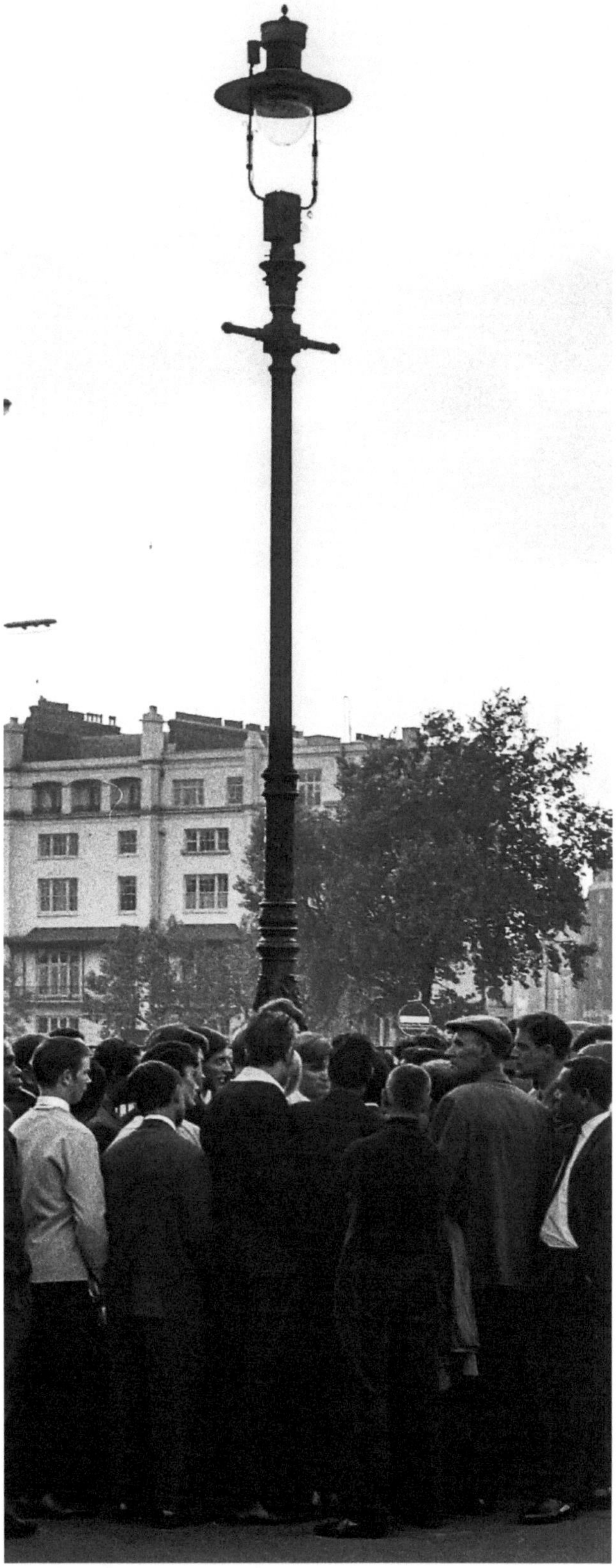

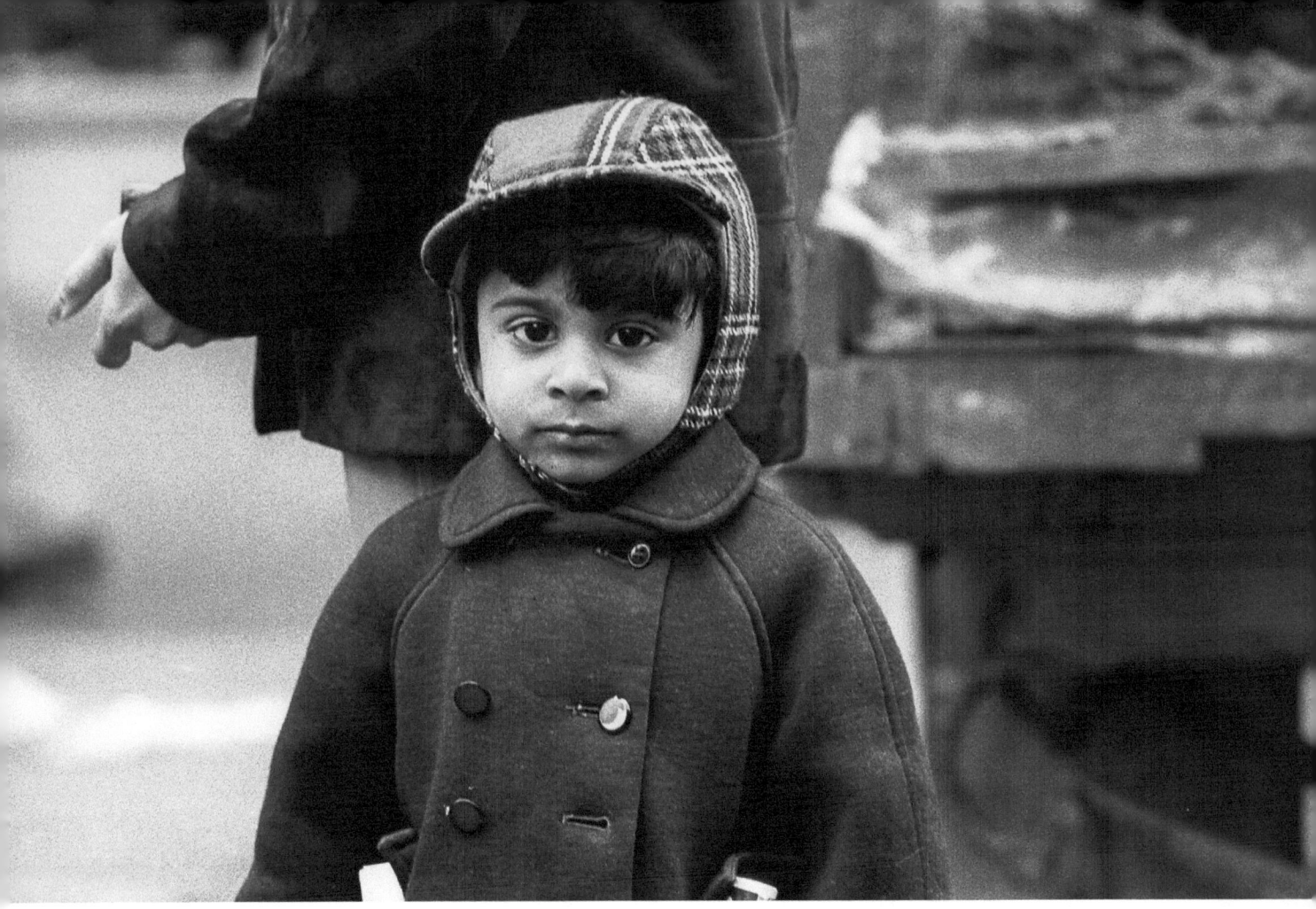

CHILDREN IN LONDON

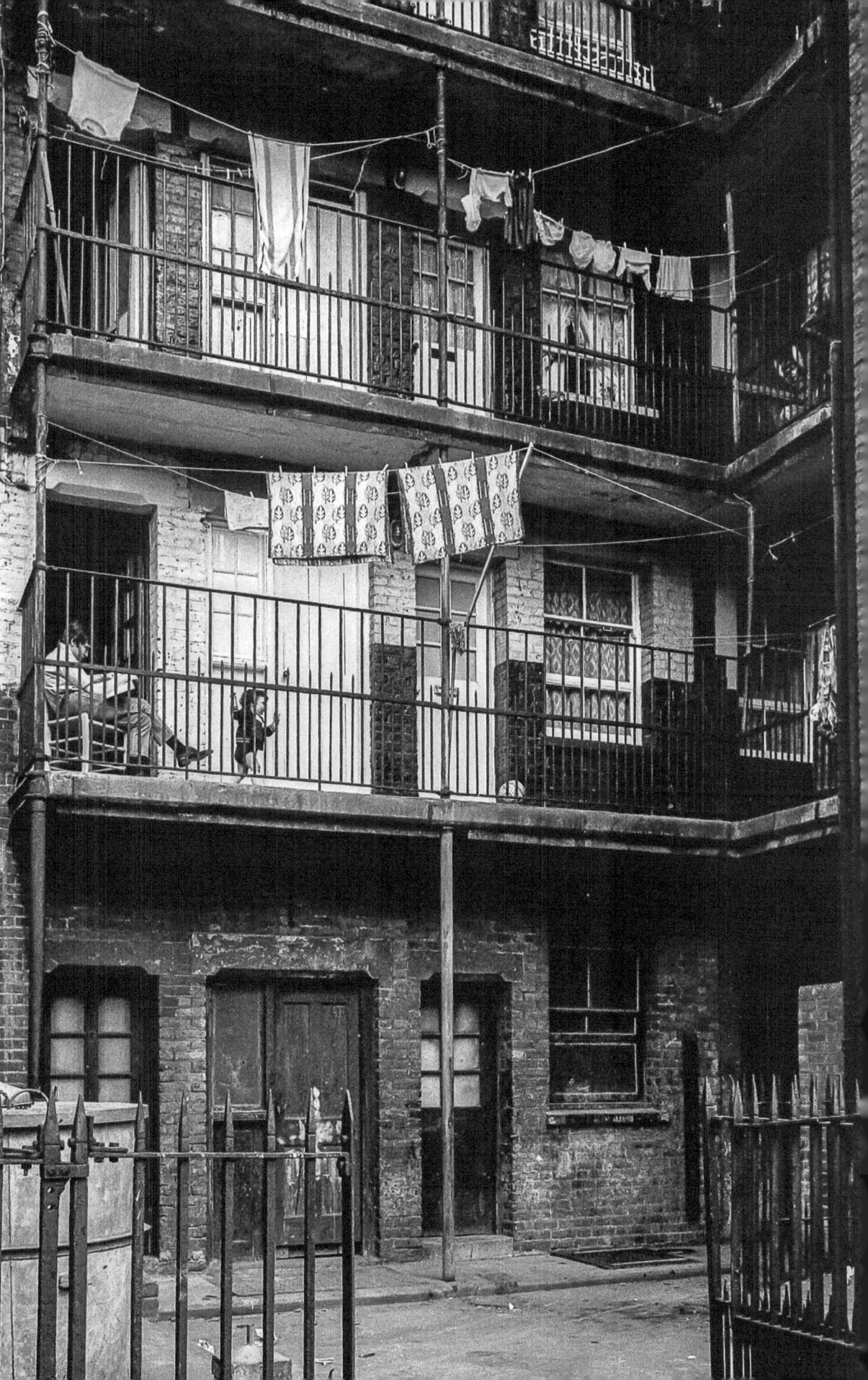

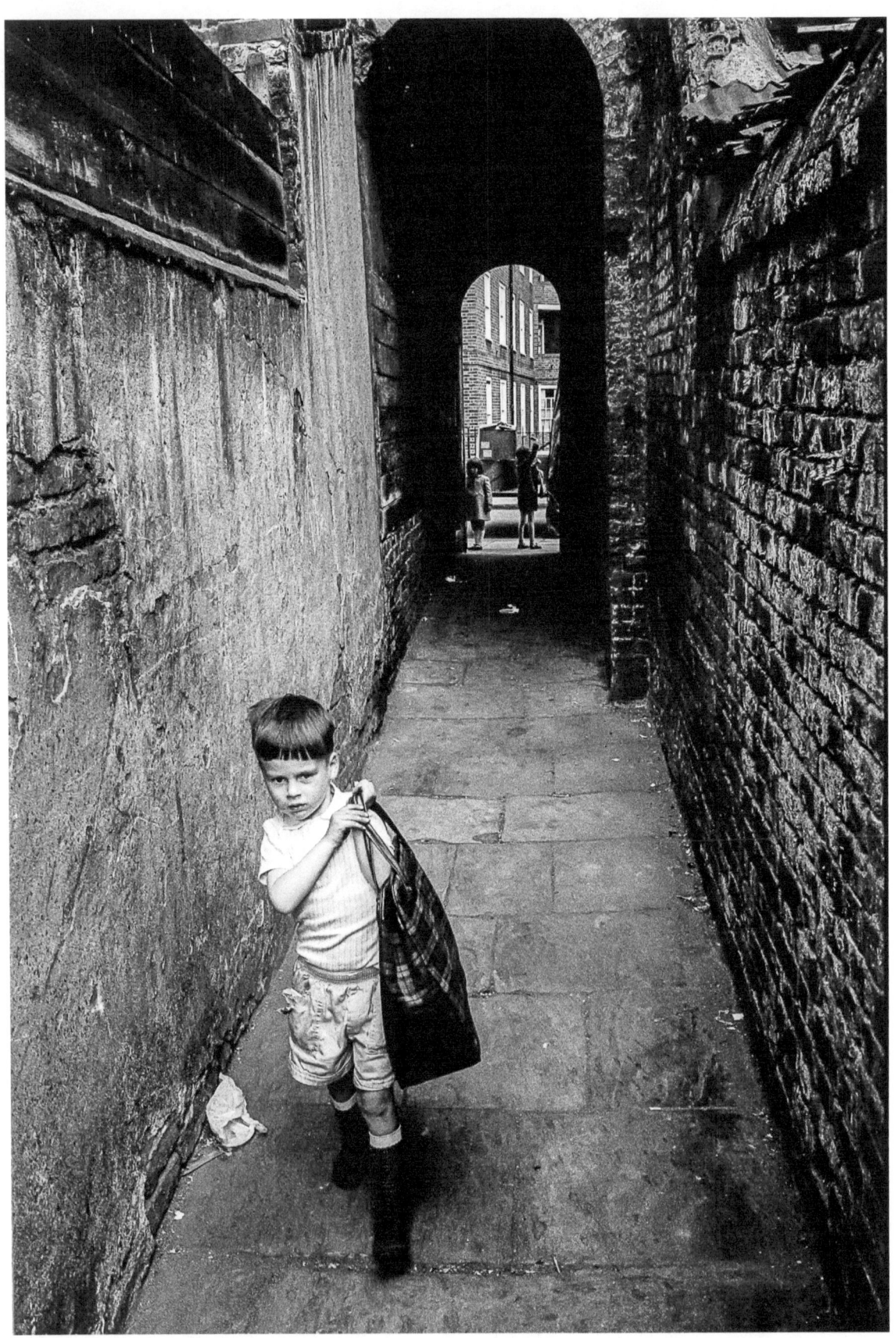

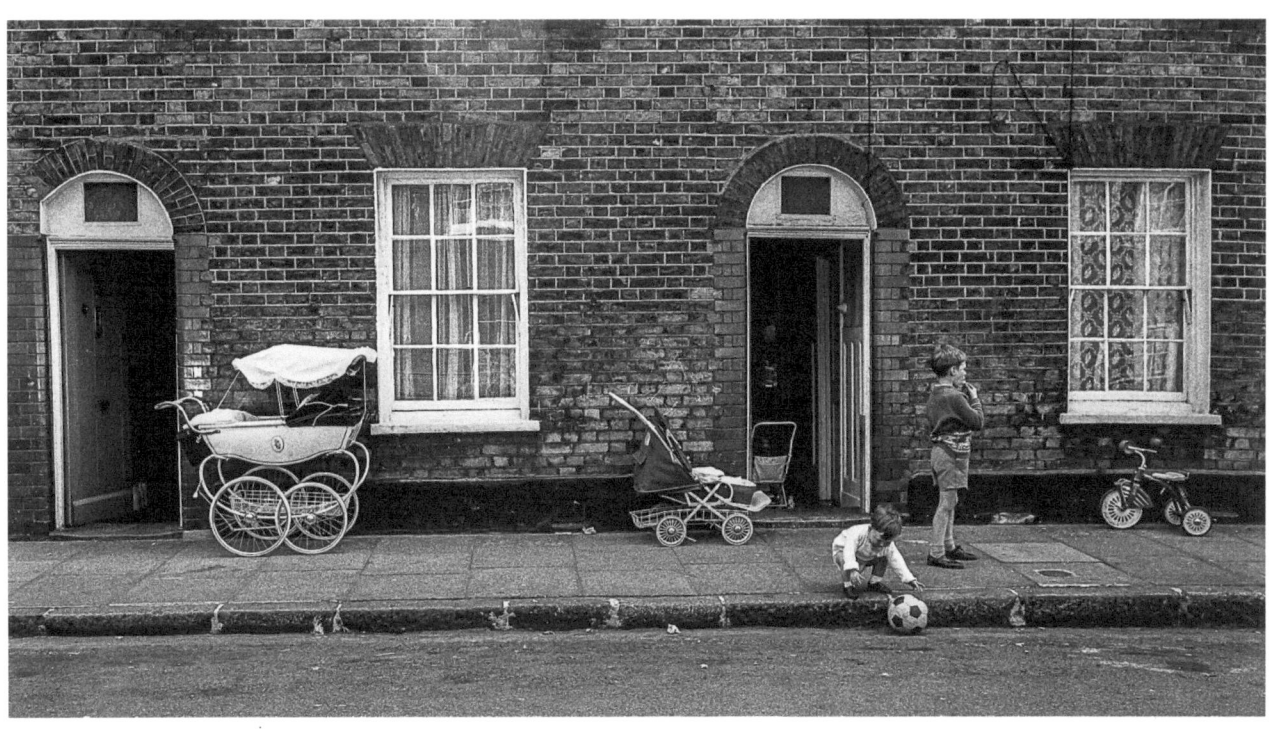

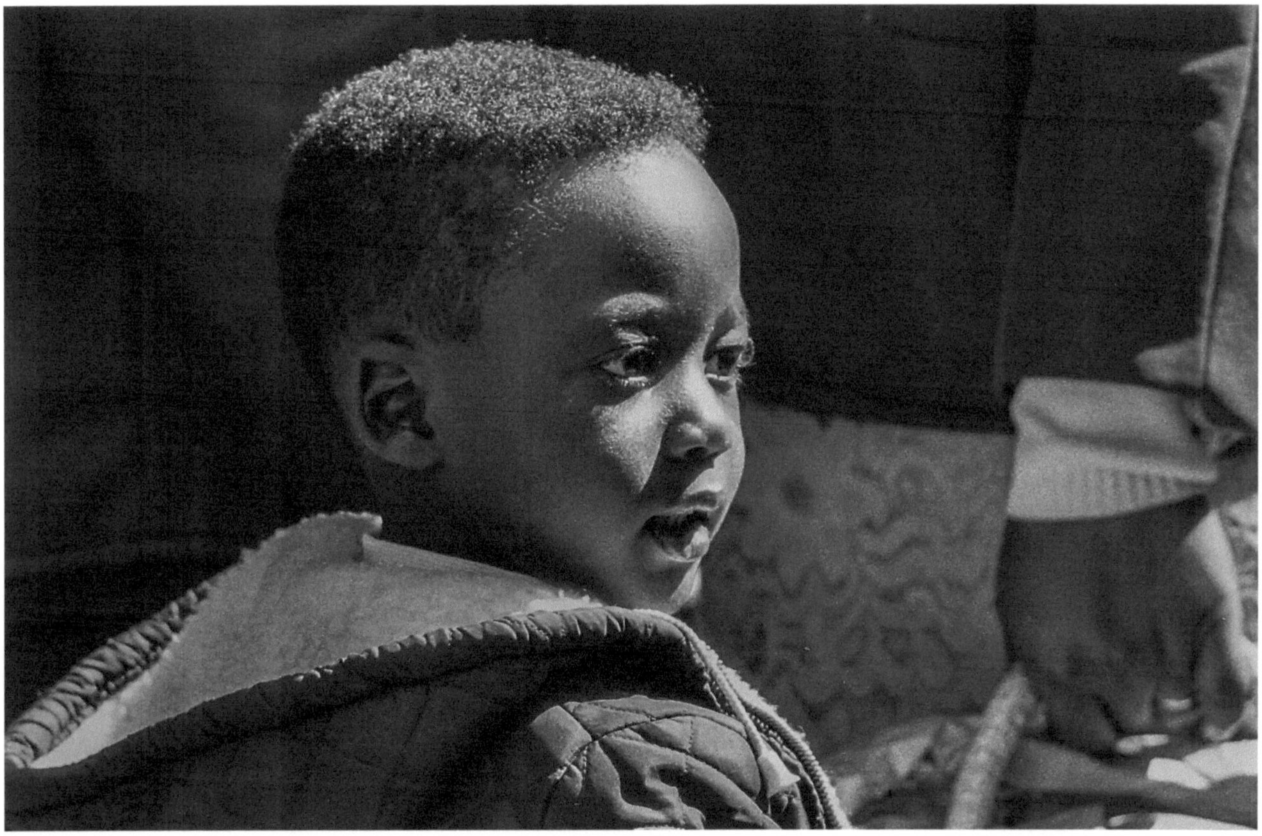

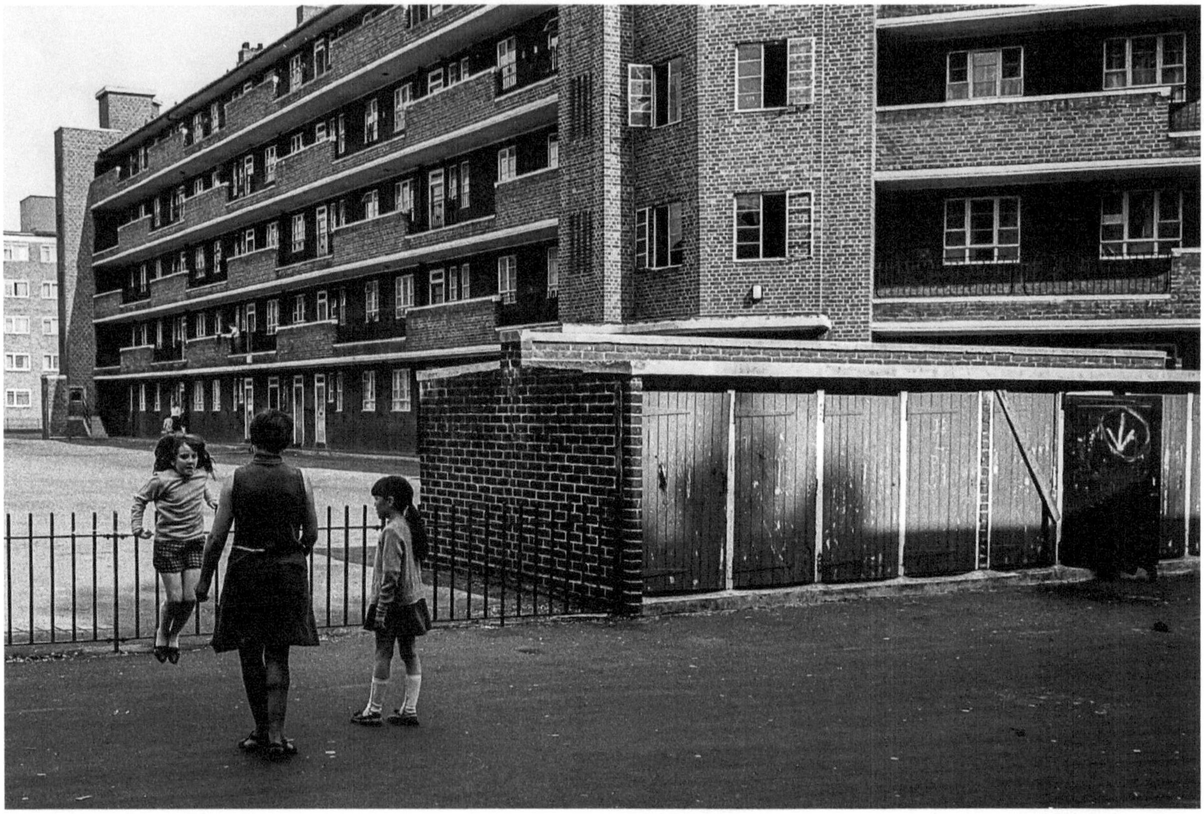

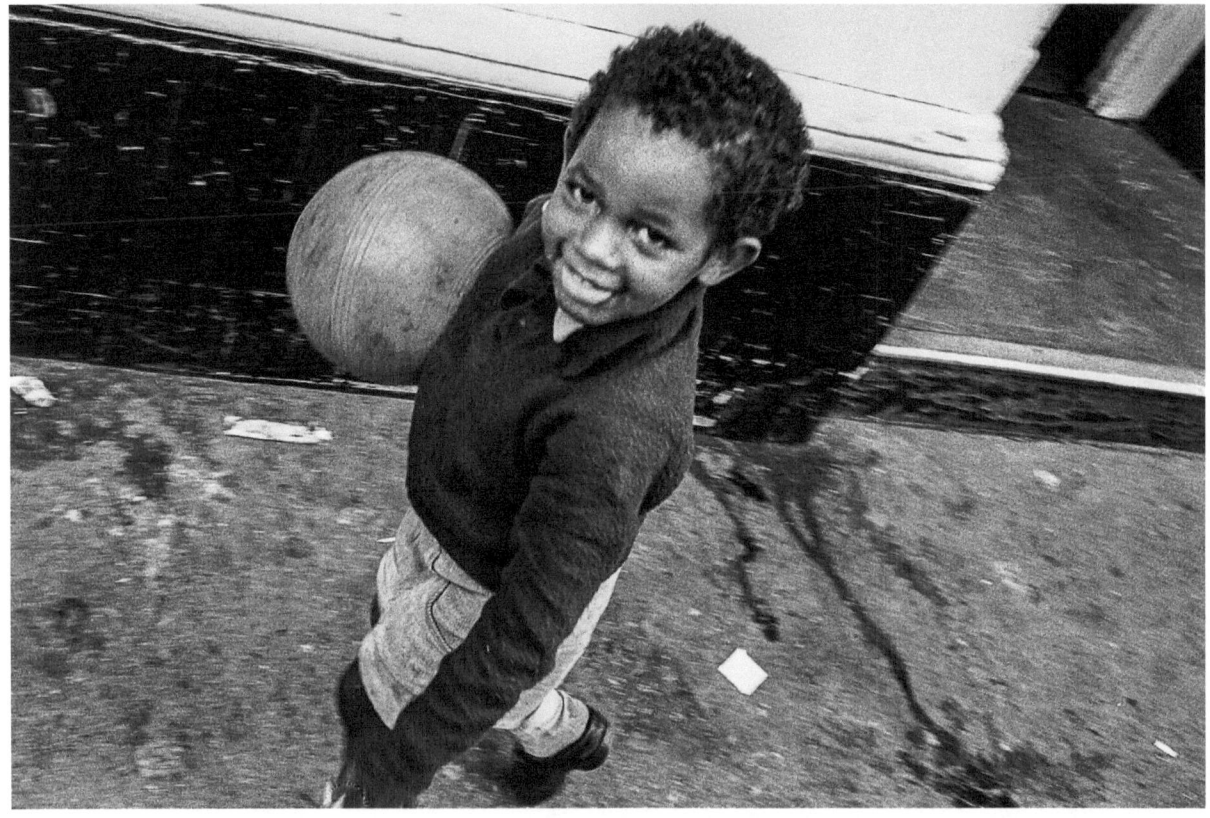

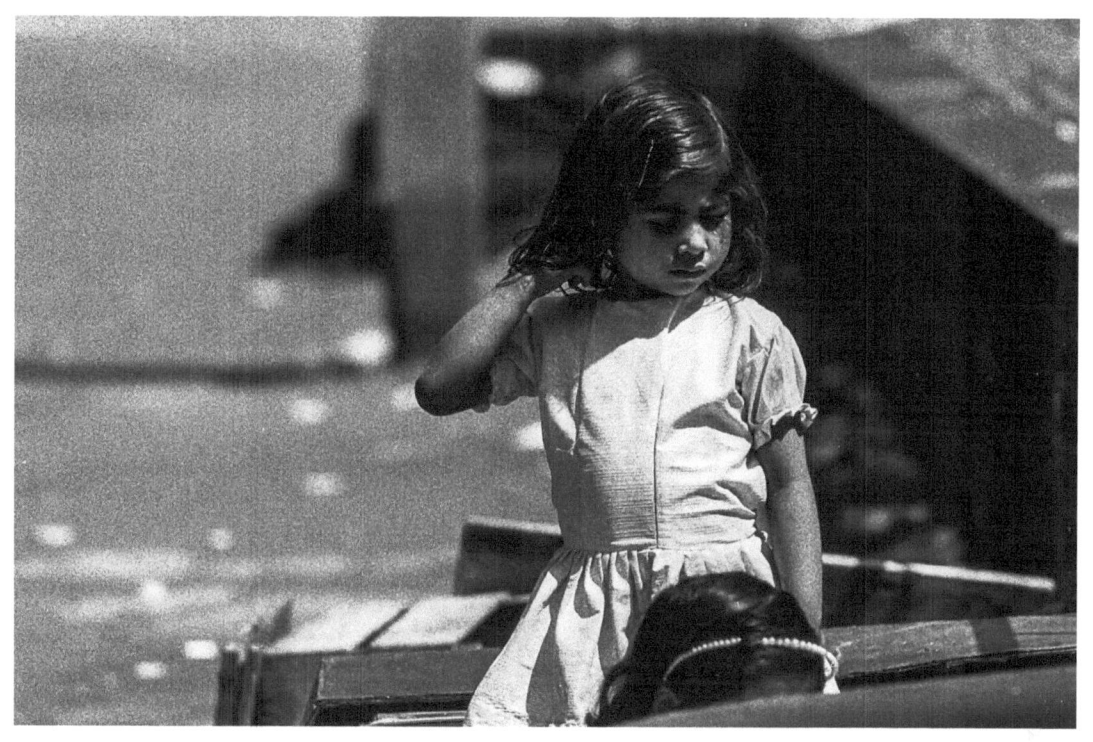

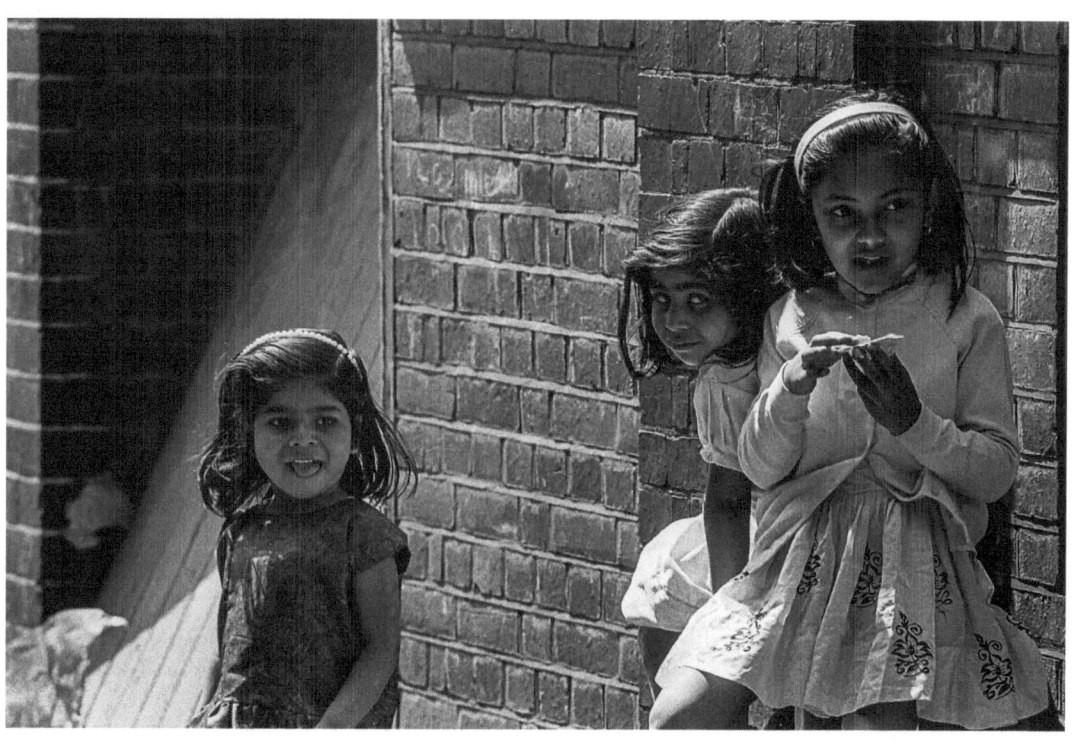

NEW CALEDONIAN MARKET

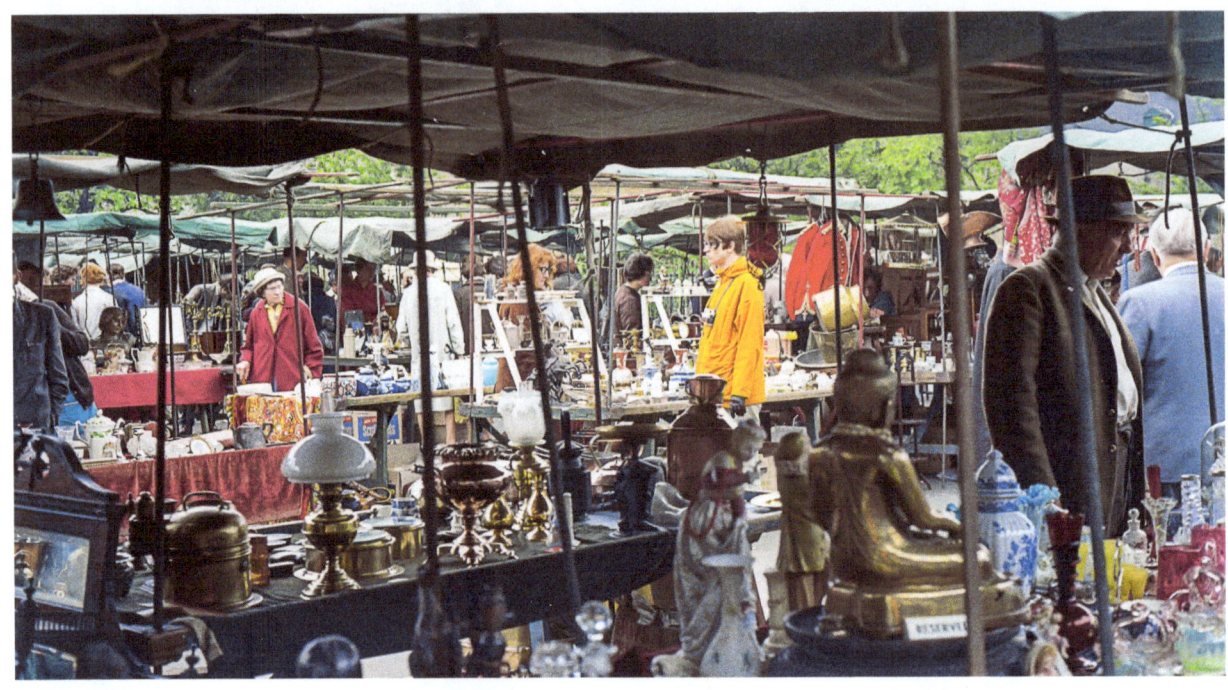

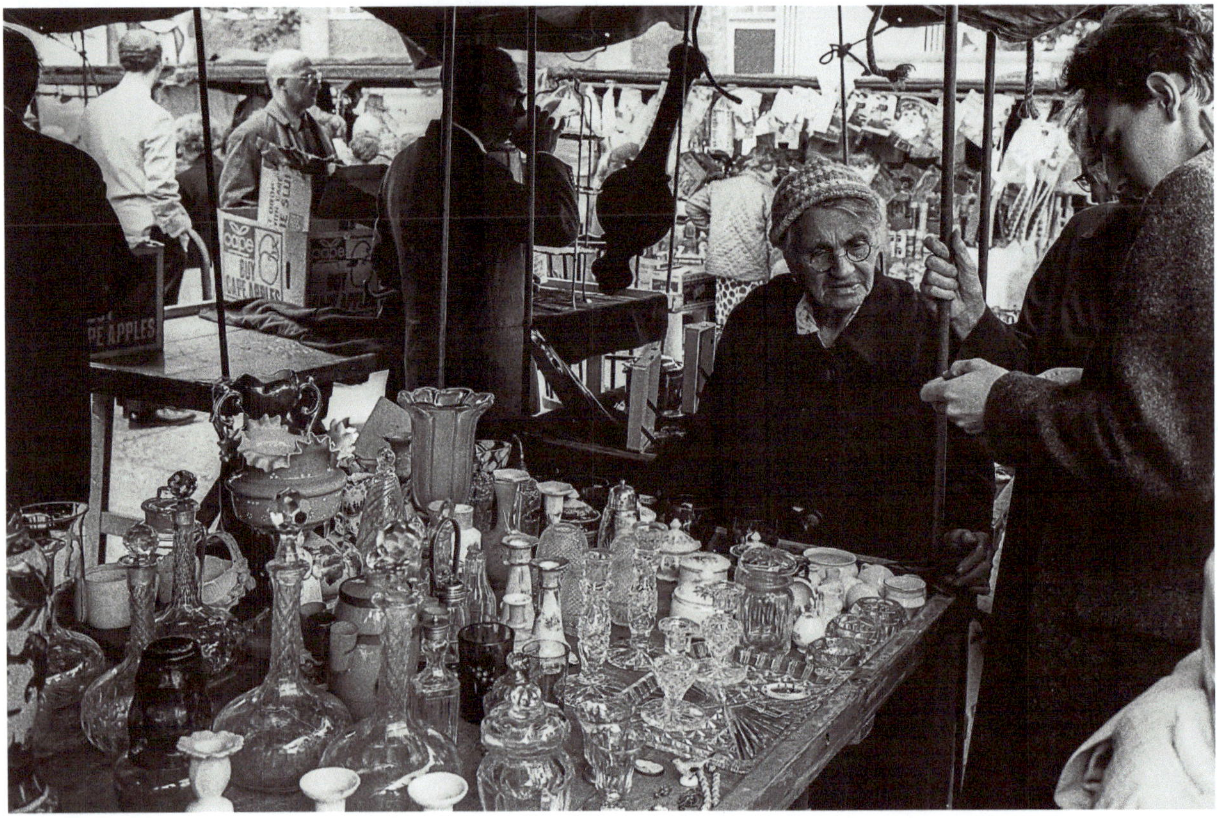

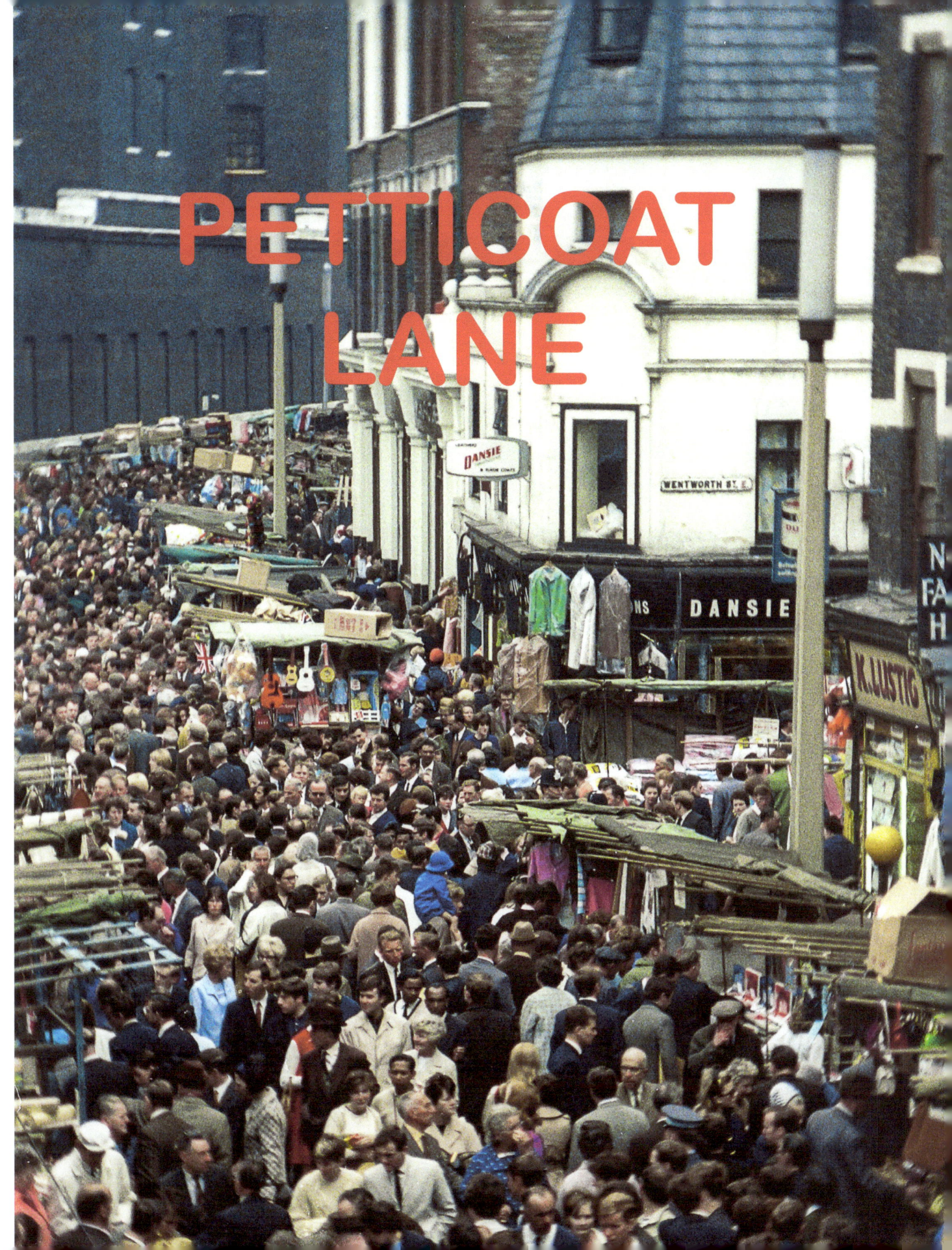

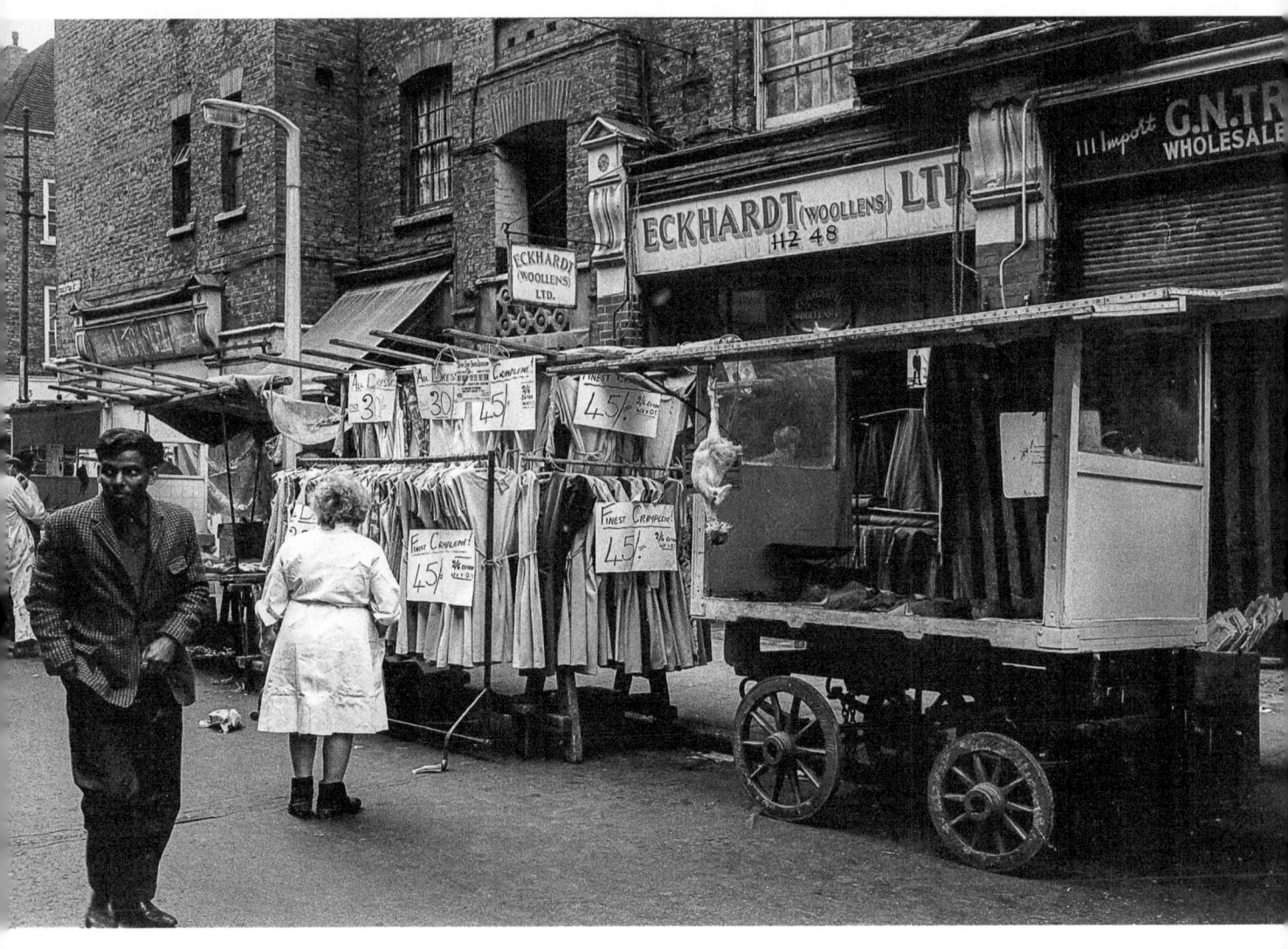

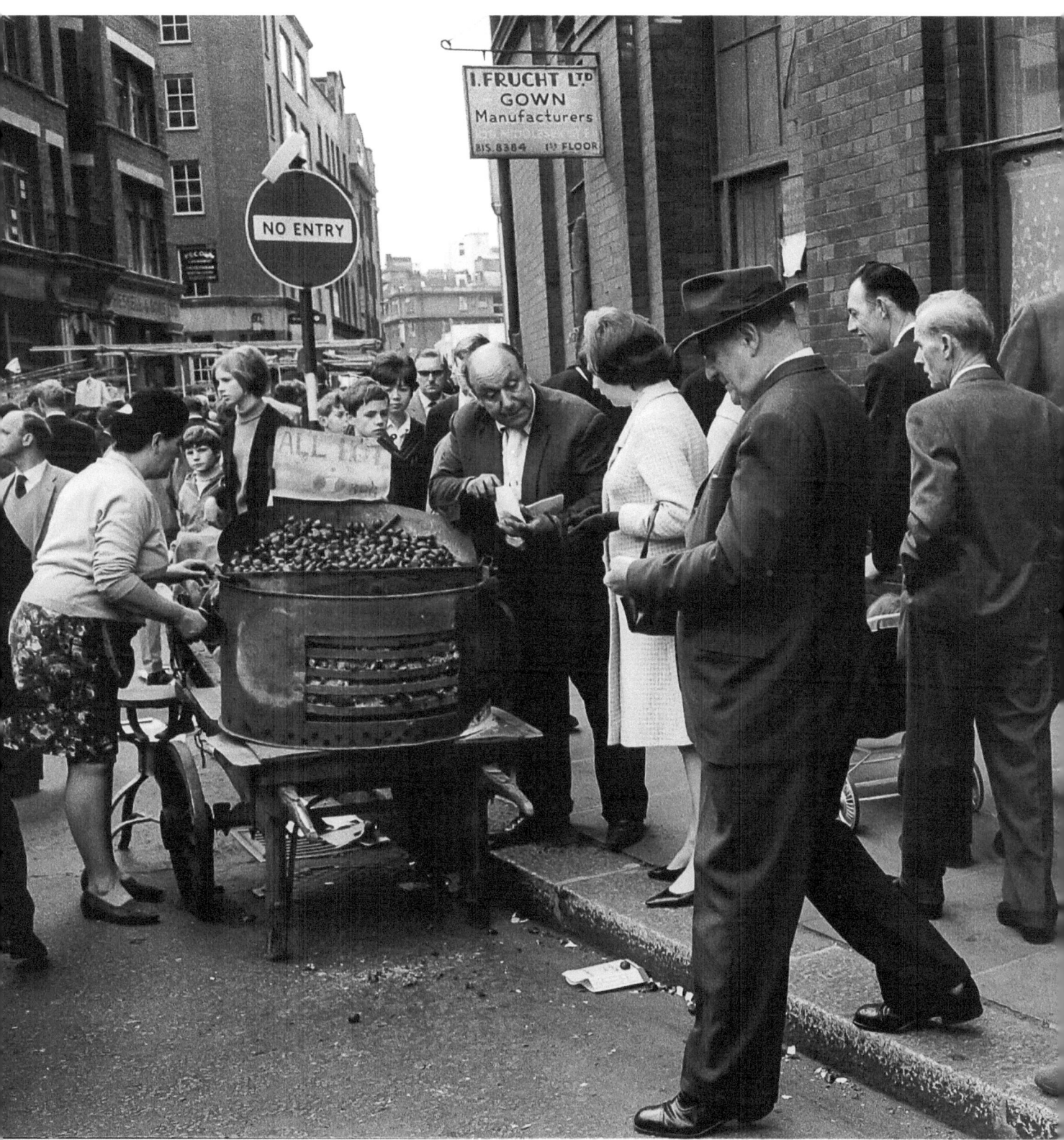

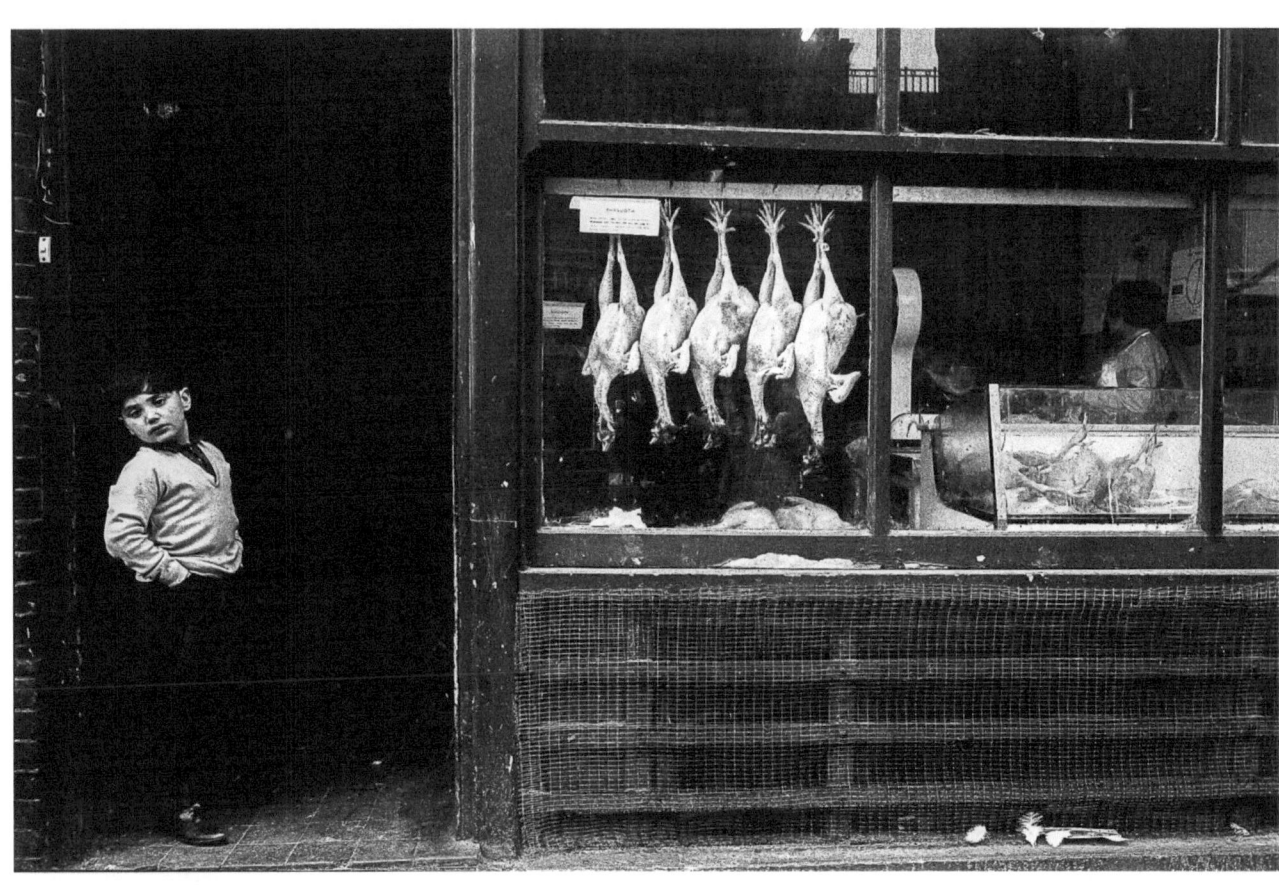

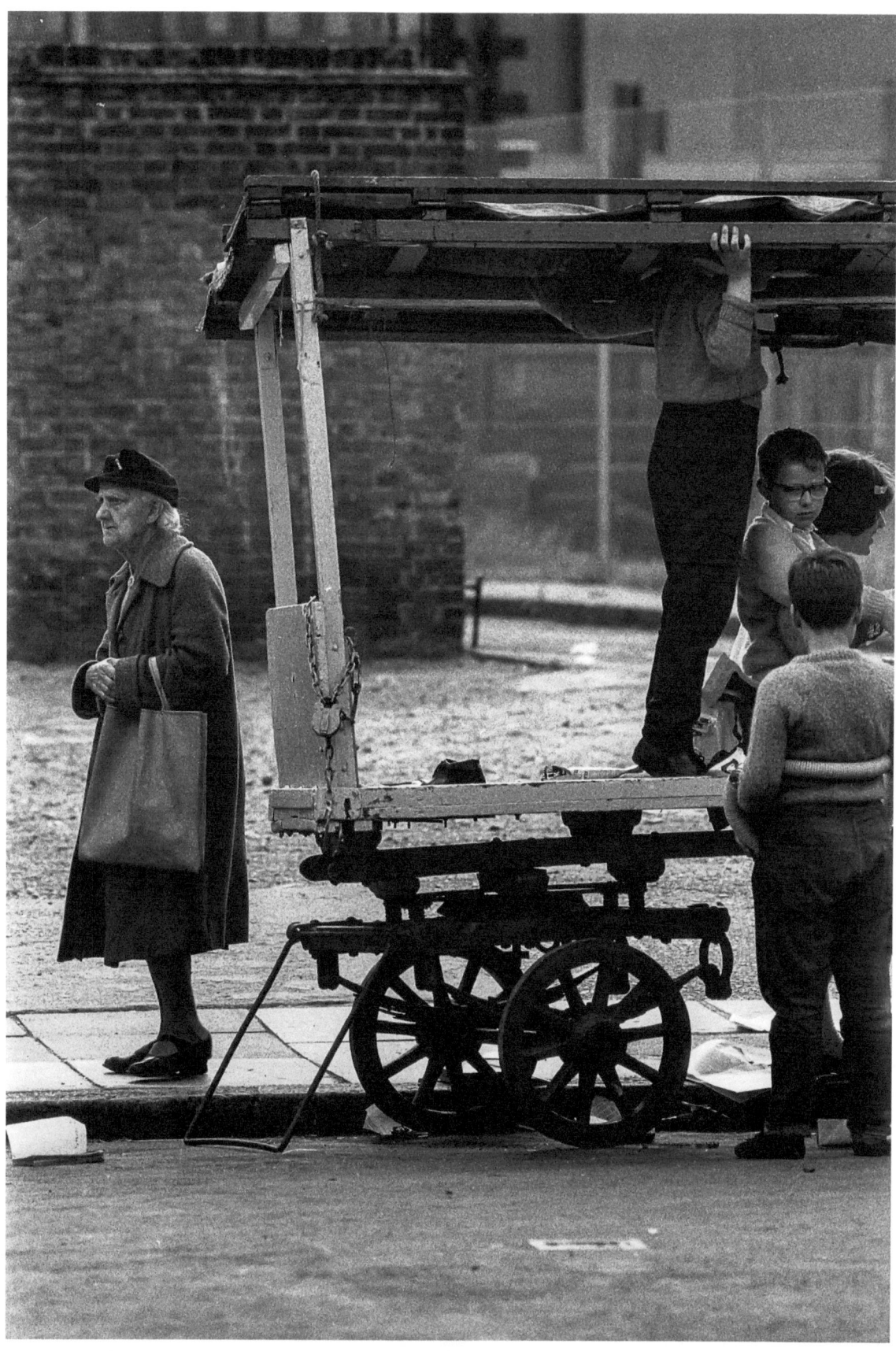

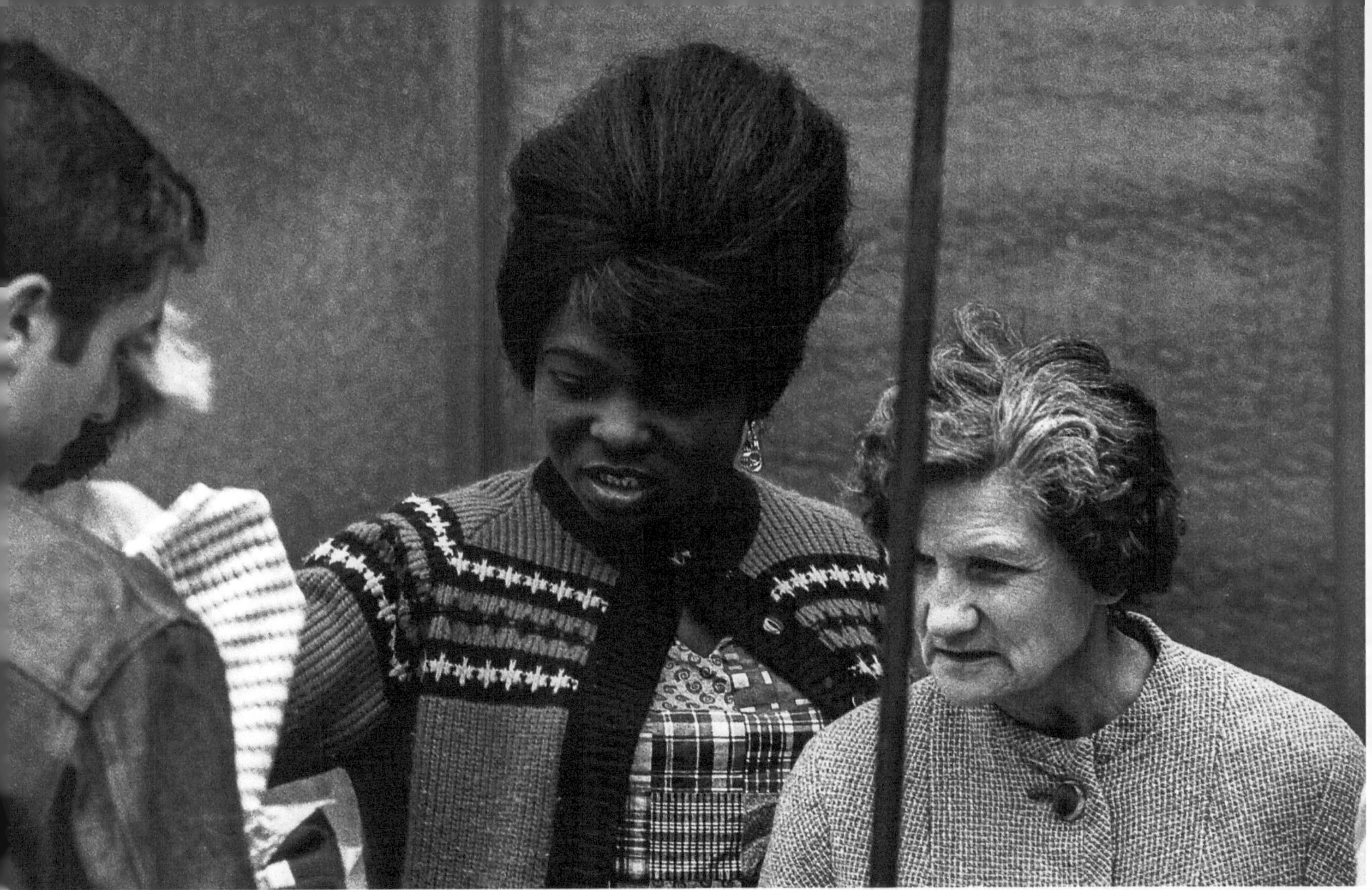

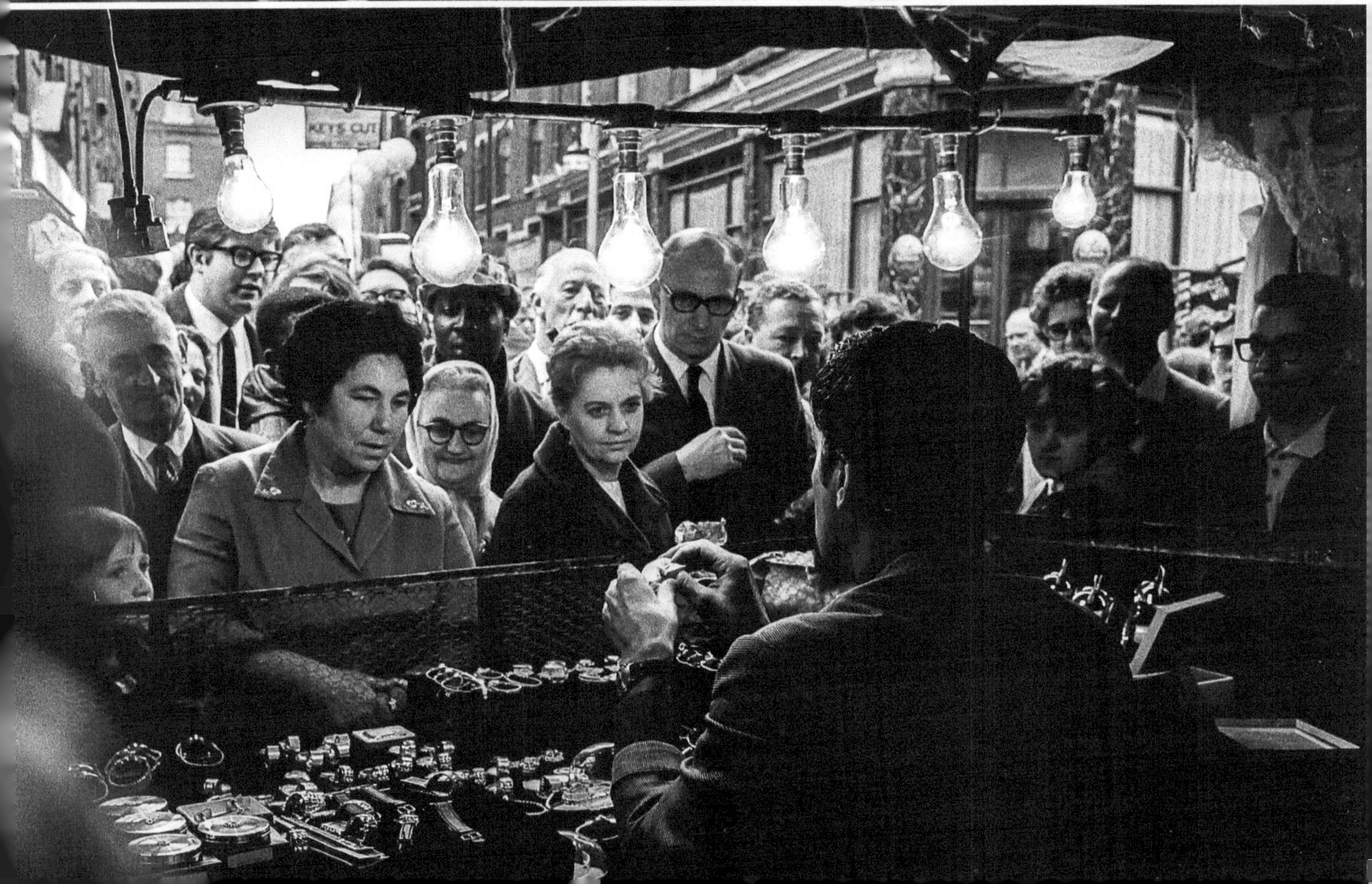

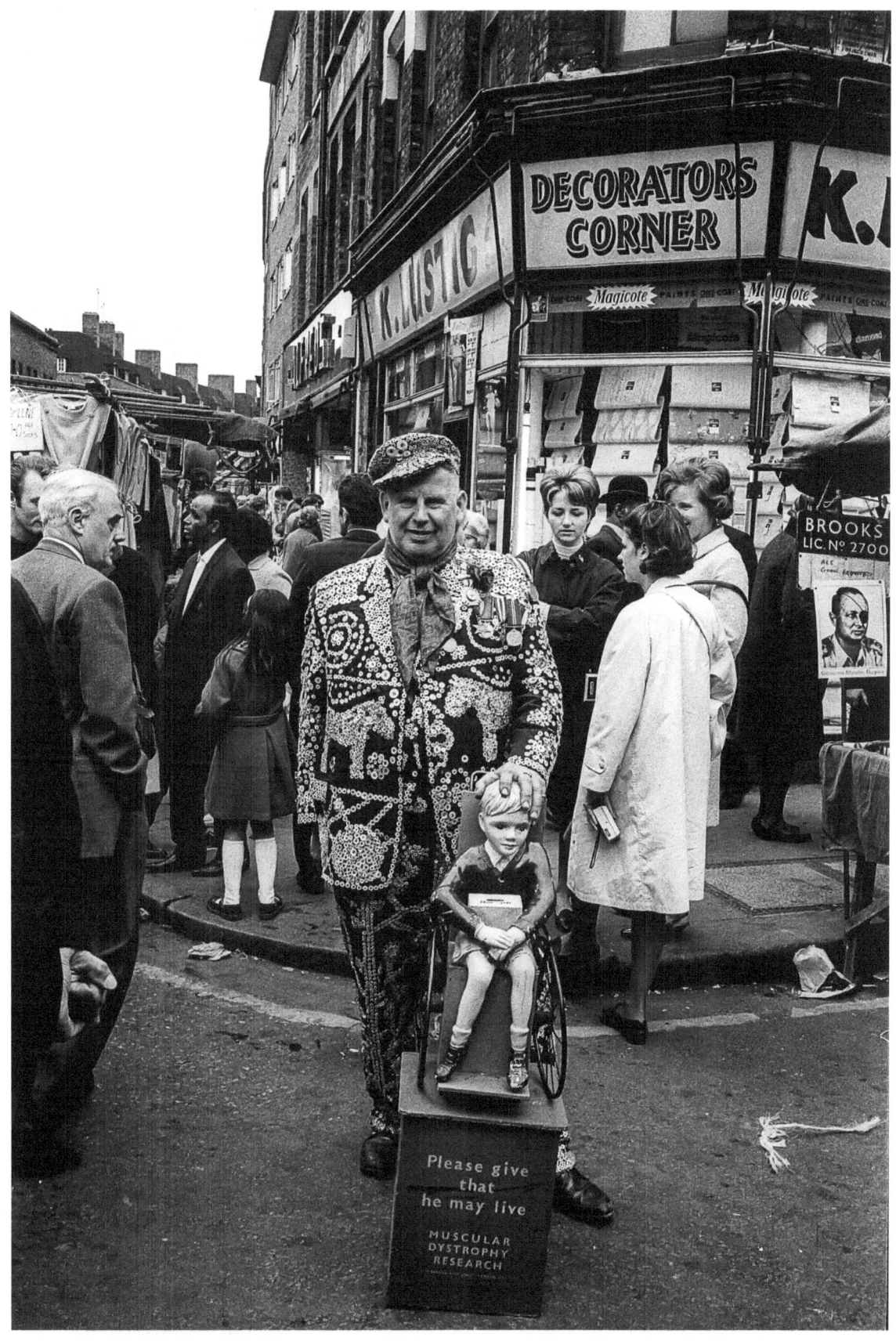

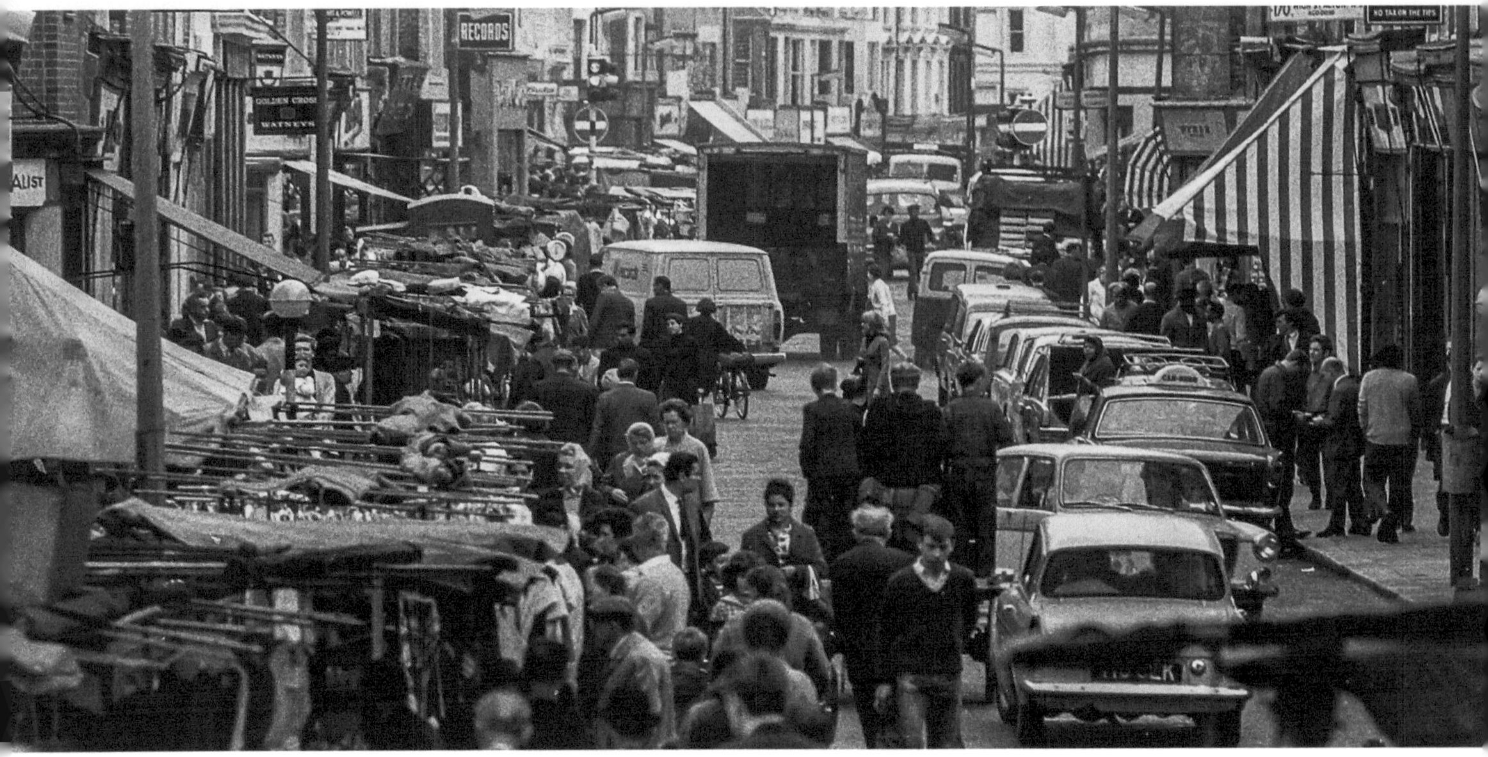

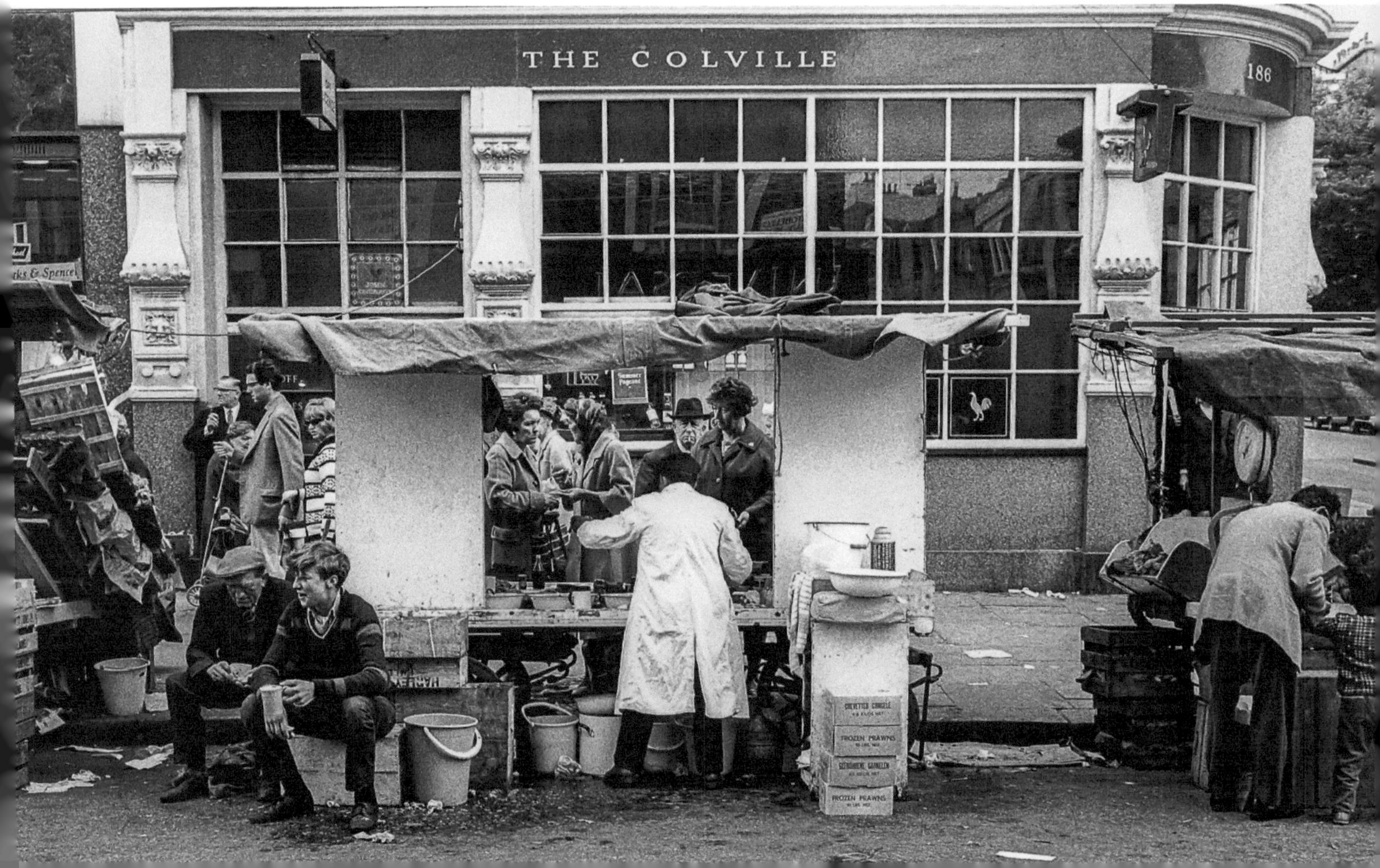

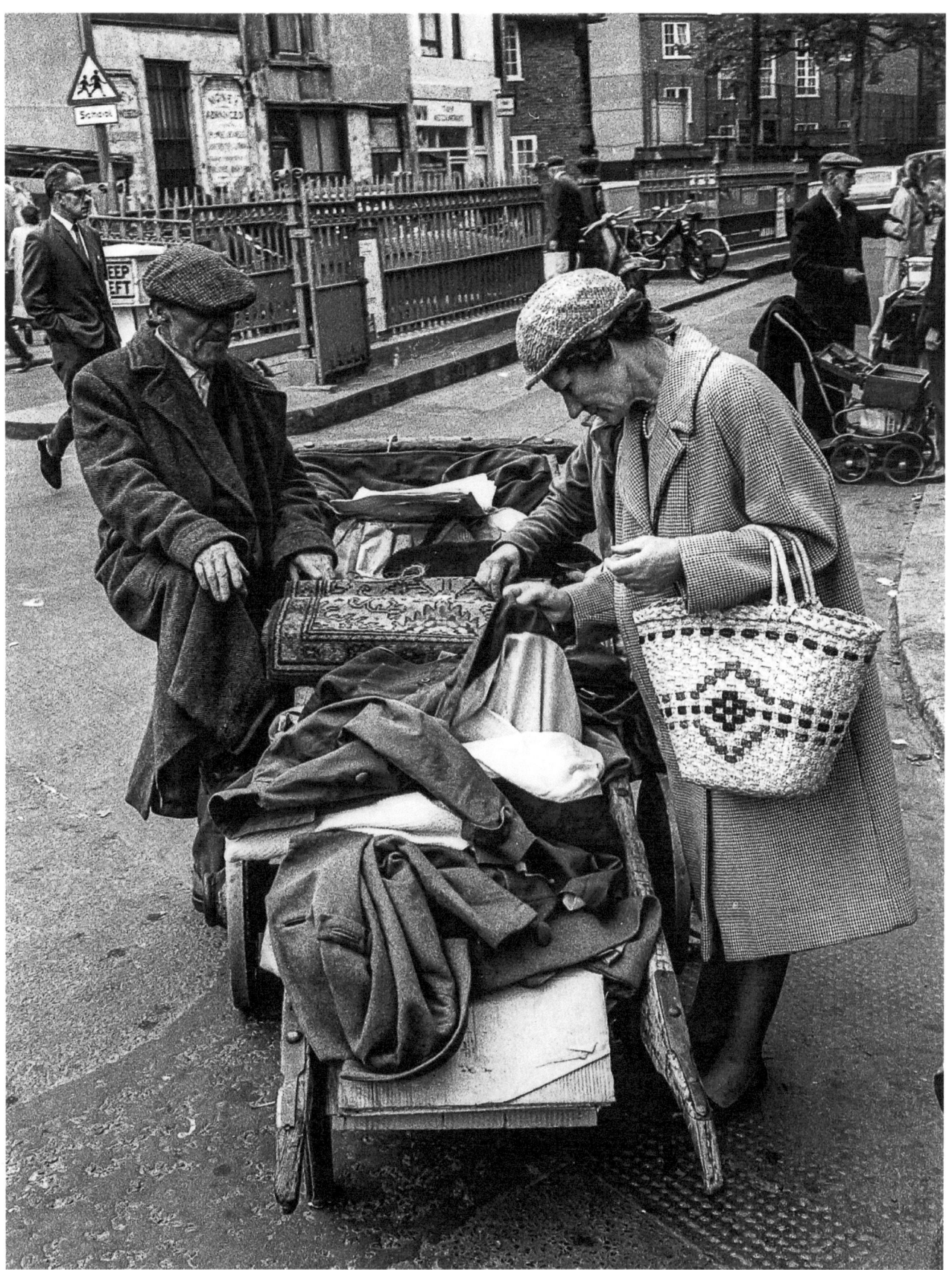

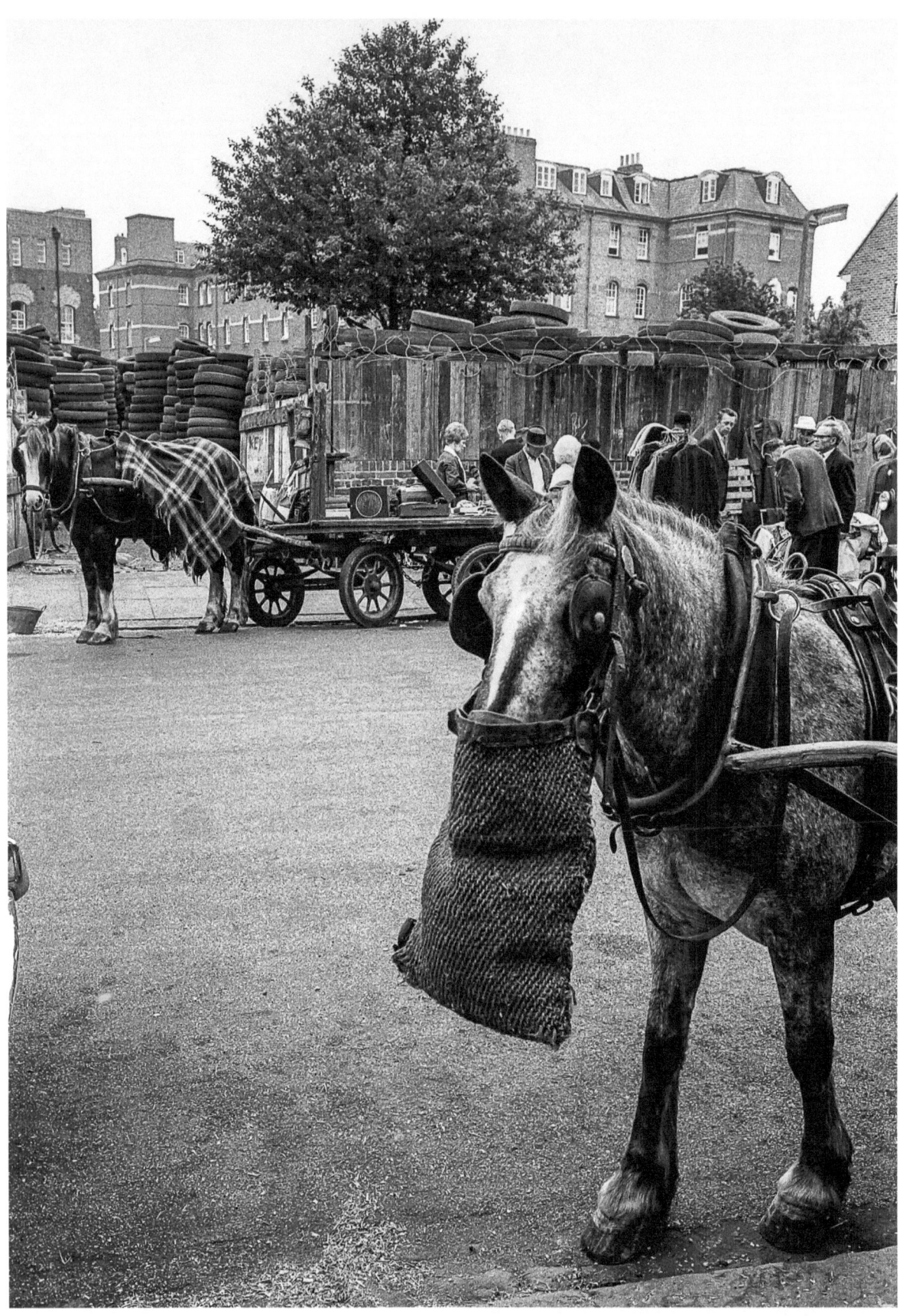

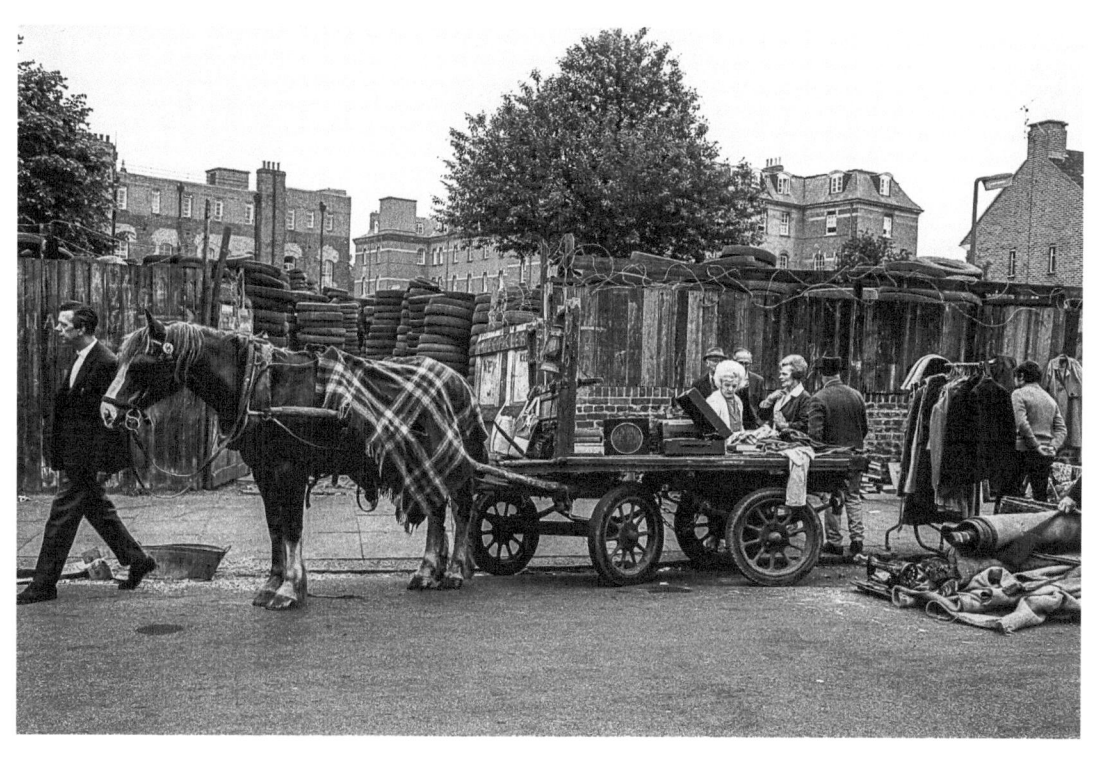

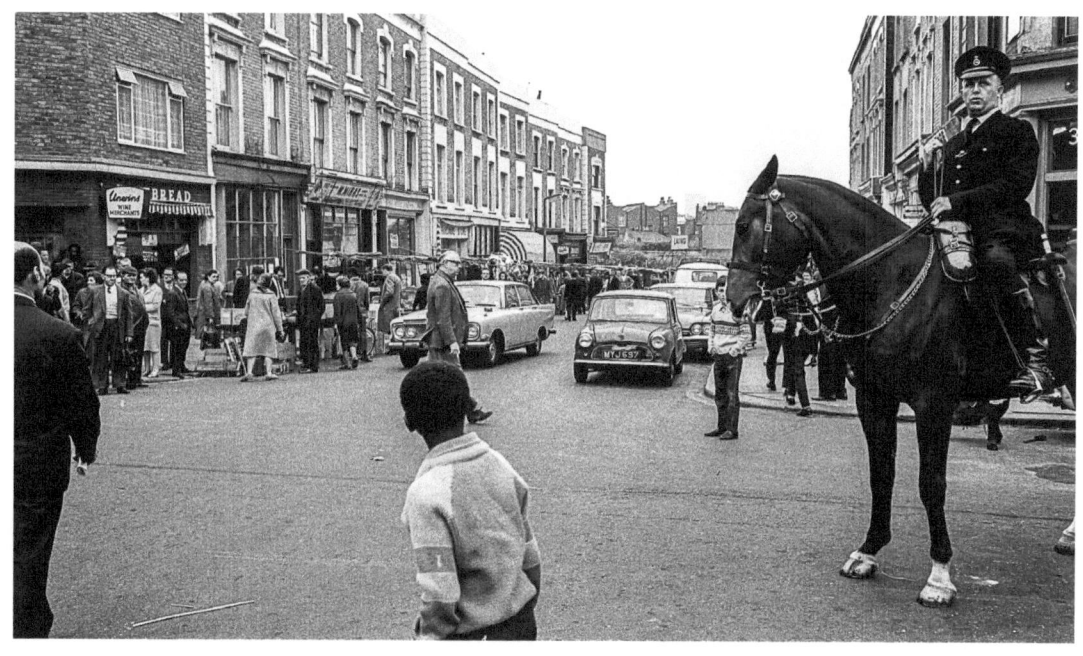

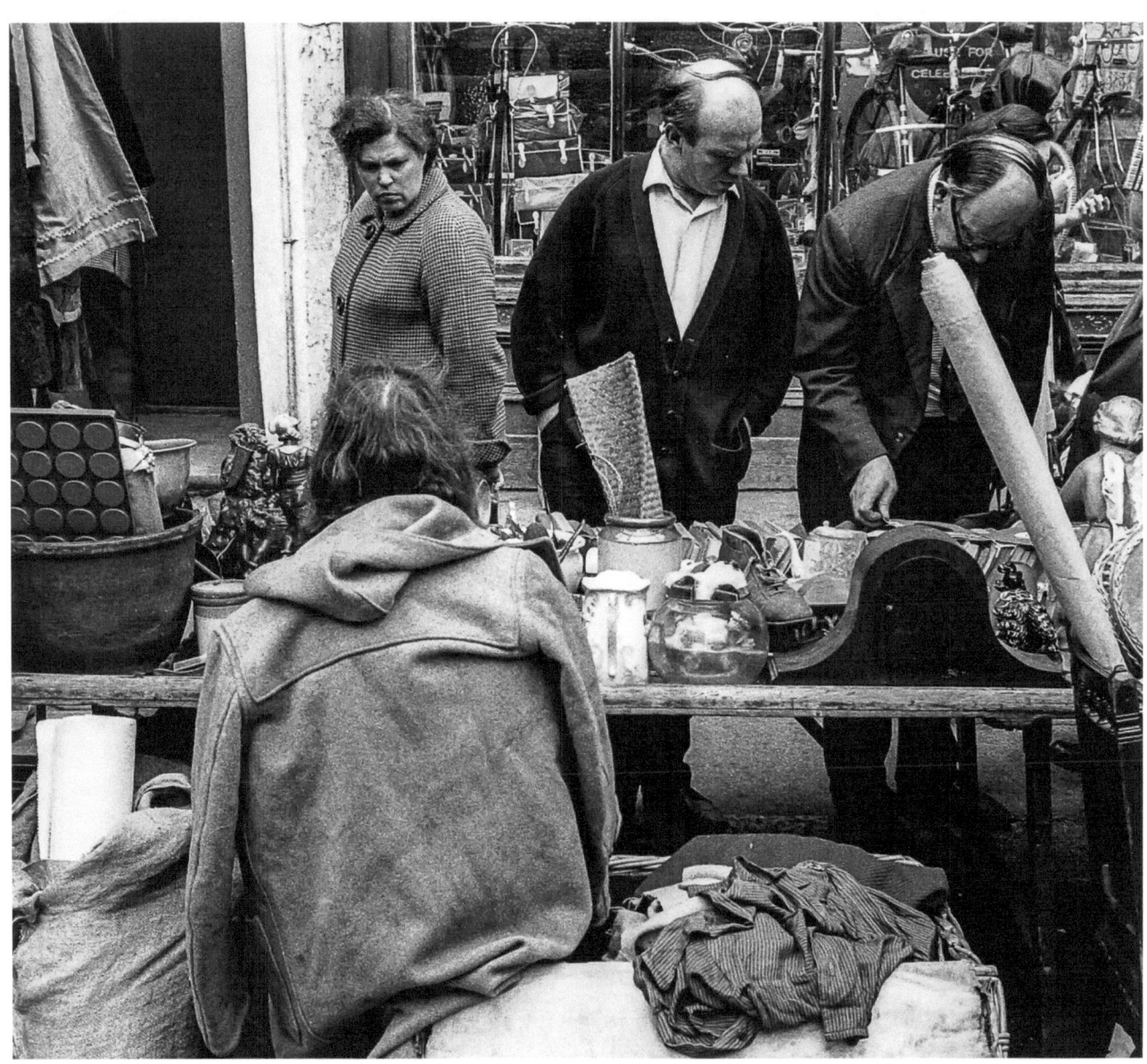

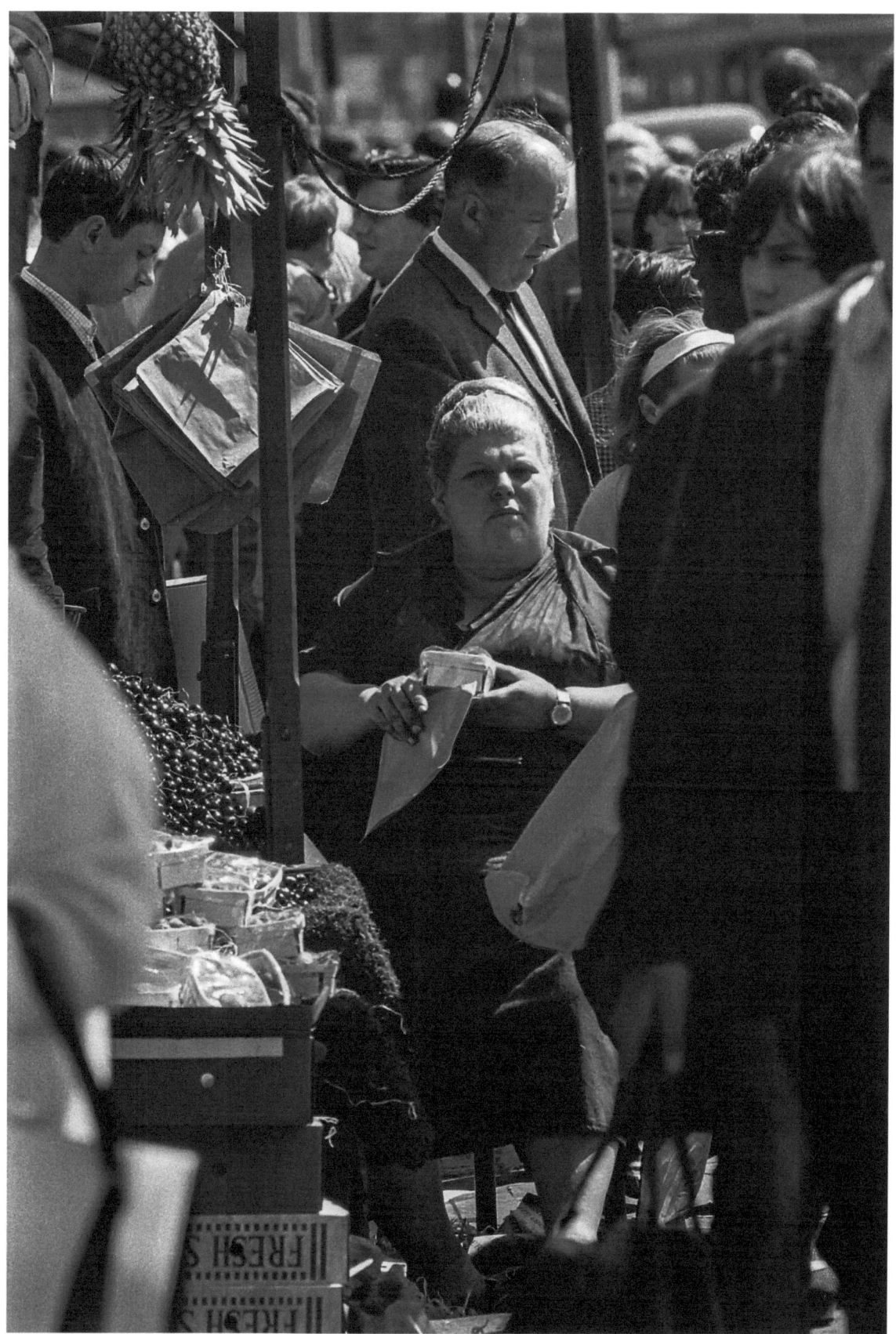

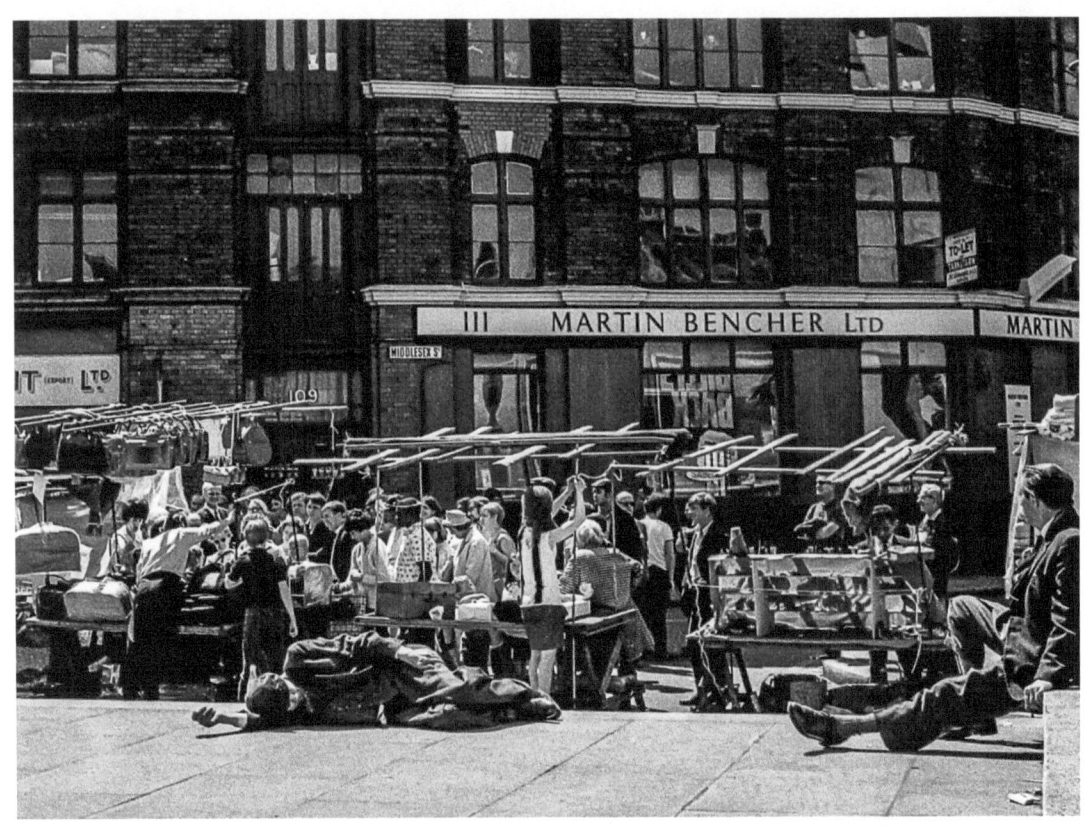
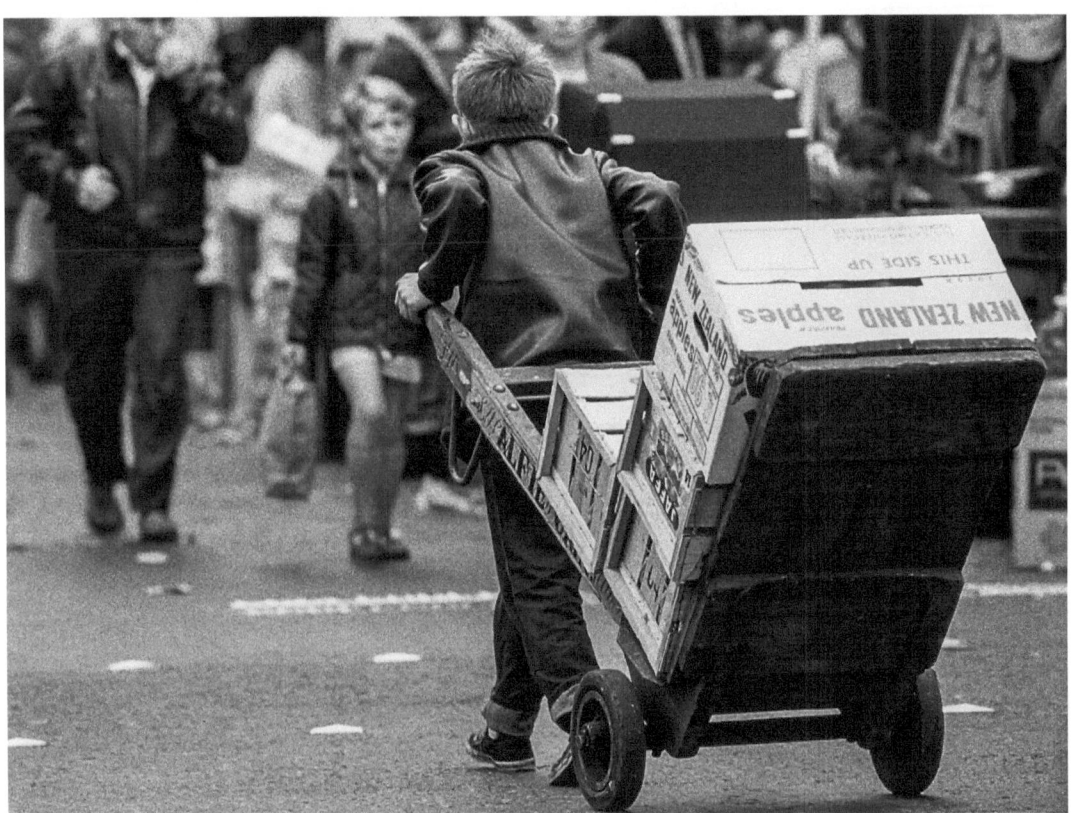

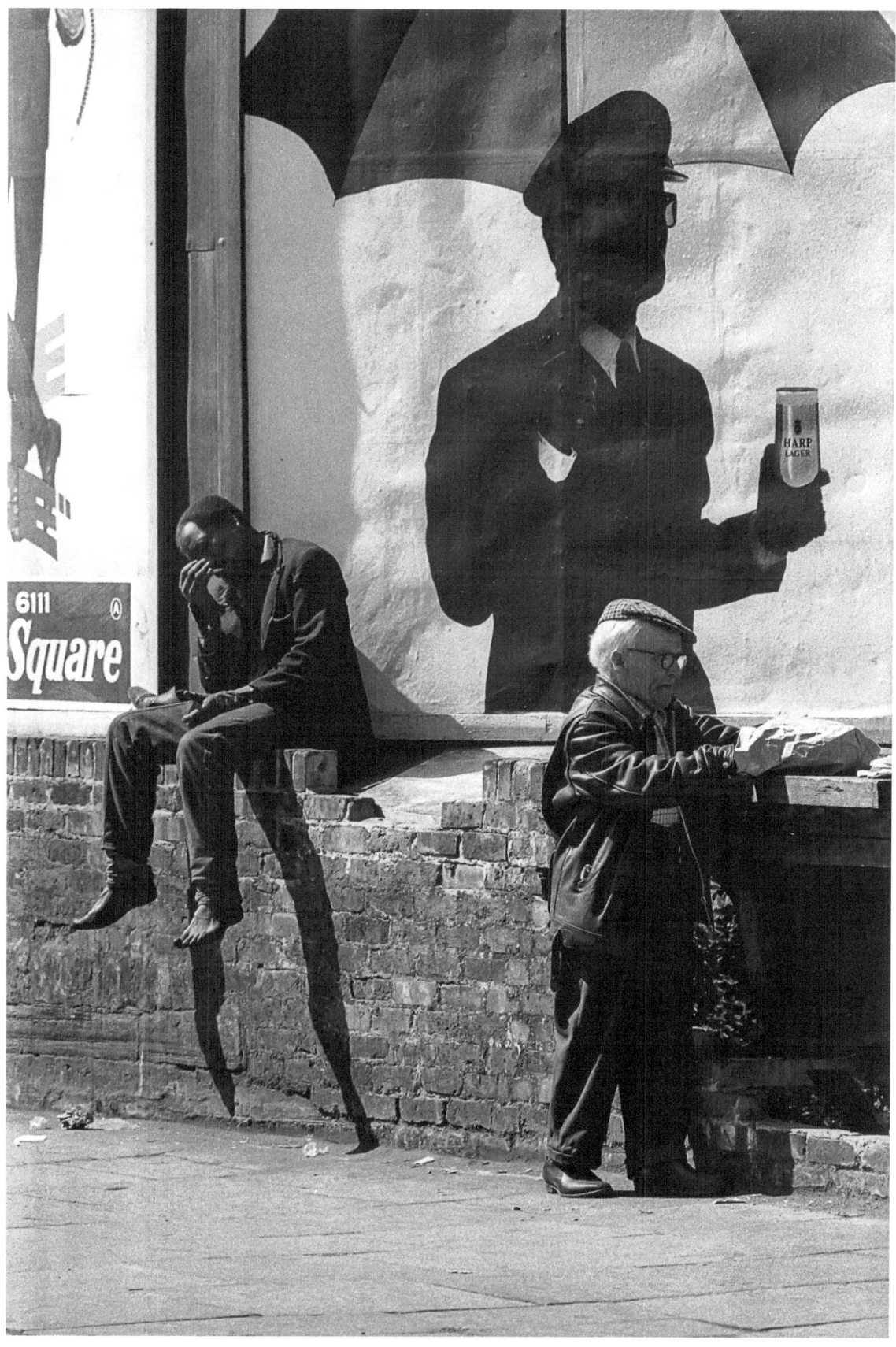

Bob and Ninni in photography

Bob has been photographing since the middle of last century. He started with an Agfa Isolette and was a 15-year-old freelance photographer at the local newspapers Corren and Östgöten. He got a picture explained best football image of the magazine Match 1958. His work as a freelance photographer aroused interest in documentary photography, which has followed Bob through life.

He and Ninni have photographed people, environments and nature on all seven continents. Today, Bob is professor emeritus at the University of Lund and is shooting photographs full time. Nowadays he publishes books, both on paper and e-books, check by Google. Bob has had solo photo exhibitions at the Östergötland County Museum and Scandinavian Photo. The most current project is to photograph polar bear and emperor penguins life on the edge of the ice, in order to highlight their role as indicators of environmental change.

Bob and Ninni have lived and worked in the Sweden, United States, France, Japan and Denmark.

Bovin Design Hb has published the following books:

New York remains. ISBN 978-1-4092-0178-6
En skola 1959. ISBN 978-91-978005-0-1
En skola 1959. e-book. ISBN 978-91-978005-1-8
Vårt skräp - framtidens fossil. e-book. ISBN 978-91-978005-2-5
Signs in situations. ISBN 978-91-978005-3-2
Humor i bilder. ISBN 978-91-978005-4-9
Humor i bilder. e-book. ISBN 978-91-978005-5-6
The Berlin Wall Falls. ISBN 978-91-978005-6-3
Berlinmurens fall. e-book. ISBN 978-91-978005-7-0
London 1967. A Photo Esaay. e-book. ISBN 978-91-978005-8-7

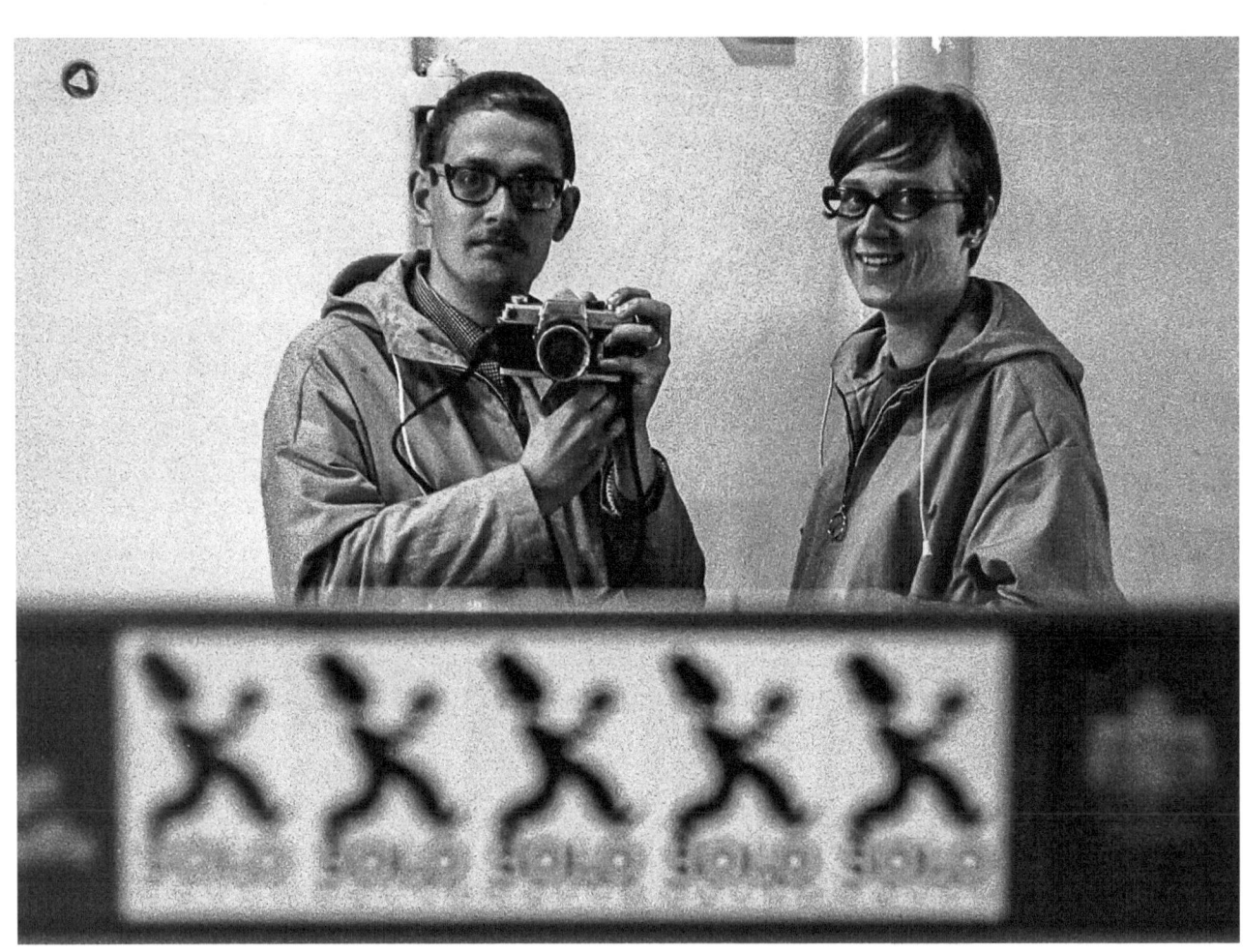

www.ingramcontent.com/pod-product-compliance
Lightning Source LLC
Chambersburg PA
CBHW051156220526
45473CB00003B/800